THE ASHES' STRANGEST MOMENTS

Extraordinary but true tales from
over a century of the Ashes

Mark Baldwin

ROBSON BOOKS

First published in Great Britain in 2005 by
Robson Books
151 Freston Road
London
W10 6TH

An imprint of Anova Books Company Ltd

ISBN 1 86105 863 2

10 9 8 7 6 5 4 3

Printed and bound by Creative Print and Design (Ebbw Vale), Wales

This book can be ordered direct from the publisher
Contact the marketing department, but try your bookshop first

Contents

Foreword by Nasser Hussain OBE

As England captain in the 2001 and 2002–03 Ashes series, I'm afraid I don't have a very long list of funny stories. In that period Australia stretched their current winning run over England to eight series – and that is not much of a laughing matter, to be honest. It is high time England reversed a trend which began in 1989, the summer before I played my own first Test match. May I wish Michael Vaughan and the England boys all the very best for this summer's 2005 Ashes series.

Cricket against the Australians of modern times has, however, been the ultimate test for those of us who have been their opponents, and it is still the pinnacle of every England cricketer's career to take part in an Ashes series. I always enjoyed pitting myself against Australia and, as can be seen from the pages of this book, matches between England and our oldest rival have provided some of the greatest moments in cricket history – as well as some of the most curious, amusing and tragic.

Two of the strangest stories I can tell from my time as England captain involve a pair of the finest innings I have ever seen played in the heat of an Ashes battle. One was by Mark Butcher at Headingley in 2001, and the other by Michael Vaughan at Adelaide in November 2002. The reason I classify both these performances as strange, by the way, is that neither was really meant to happen.

Butcher would not have played in that Headingley Test but for a last-minute change of heart by myself and the England management. During the previous match, Mark had been spotted out and about much, much later than was acceptable on the evening of a Test – in an expedition that also probably involved a couple of Jack Daniels and Cokes – and initially it was decided to discipline him by leaving him out at Leeds. We were 3–0 down at the time, too, after three Tests, so tolerance levels were wearing a bit thin.

David Fulton of Kent was actually selected for what would have been his Test debut, but then we began to have second thoughts. I rang around a few people, like Alec Stewart and Mike Atherton, and the general consensus was that dropping 'Butch' was a little harsh. In the end, he was merely read the riot act by Duncan Fletcher and myself and fined £1,000. And he went out at the end of that Headingley Test and won England the match with an unbeaten 173 that will probably stand as the best innings of his career.

Vaughan himself was about ten seconds away from not being included in the England team to play the second Test of the 2002–03 series in Adelaide. He was already suffering from knee trouble, and he hurt the joint again warming up before the game. It looked as if he had no chance of playing, but he went off for treatment just in case. We had several other injury problems in the squad at that time – as seemed always to be the case in the Ashes Tests of my era – and so an emergency message was sent out to Ian Blackwell of Somerset, who was with the National Academy squad based in Adelaide that winter.

Blackwell's name was on my official team list as I set out to walk to the pitch to toss up with Steve Waugh before the start of the game – and Vaughan's was not. But, as I stepped on to the grass, I got a frantic signal from the dressing room to indicate that Michael was OK after all. That enabled me, just, to scribble in his name in place of Blackwell's before I reached the middle. What then happened, inevitably, was that after I won the toss and decided to bat, Vaughany went out and scored a quite magnificent 177 in the day – almost on one leg.

The majority of my most amusing Ashes memories inevitably involve Darren Gough, although I wasn't selected for the Ashes tour of 1994–95 in which Phil Tufnell ended up on a psychiatrist's couch in Perth for an hour or so before discharging himself, ending up running out of the hospital with the staff chasing after him.

Goughie, of course, is also an absolutely priceless character – in a completely different way to Tuffers. On the first day of the 1997 Ashes series, at Edgbaston, when we bowled Australia out for 118 to set up a great victory, I remember his reaction when a call of no ball denied him the wicket of Greg Blewett.

We were all distraught, as our wild celebrations were cut short by the umpire's signal, but Goughie just didn't seem bothered at all. 'I'll get him out again next ball instead,' he announced, before bouncing back to the end of his run. And, do you know what, he did – caught by me in the slips!

Darren also made us laugh when he took his famous hat-trick in the Sydney Test during the 1998–99 Ashes tour. The hat-trick ball was an unplayable outswinging yorker which beat Colin Miller all ends up and removed his off stump. Fantastic stuff . . . except that Goughie had forecast to us all that he was going to bowl an inswinger. But when it went the other way, he tried to insist to everyone that he meant it!

But what is perhaps Goughie's greatest moment came, thankfully, in front of several of his England team-mates outside an Australian nightclub in the early days of the 2002–03 tour – before he had to fly home with a recurrence of his knee problems. Confronted by a burly bouncer who didn't seem too keen to let Gough and his mates in, England's finest piped up: 'Hey, don't you know who I am? I took a hat-trick against you Australians in the Test match at Sydney four years ago – I'm Darren Gough!' The bouncer, however, didn't seem too impressed, and Goughie never did manage to talk his way through the door.

This book – which provides a fascinating alternative look at the wonderful history of the Ashes – is full of many better stories than that. But I must admit that particular tale still tickles me whenever one of the other lads who was there with Goughie reminds me of it!

Nasser Hussain played in 96 Tests for England from 1990 to 2004, scoring 5,764 runs and captaining his country in 45 of those matches. He scored 71 and 47 not out in his debut Ashes Test, at Trent Bridge in 1993, and appeared overall in five

Ashes series. In his 23 Ashes Test matches he made 1,581 runs at an average of 38.56, including eleven half-centuries and two centuries. One of those hundreds was actually converted into a double ton, and Hussain has always rated that 207 at Edgbaston in 1997 as his greatest Test innings. His fourteenth Test hundred was also the last innings of his career; immediately after his match-winning 103 not out against New Zealand at Lord's in May 2004 he retired to work in the media.

Introduction

There is a kind of Homeric quality to the epic story of the Ashes, but I hope I am not offending classicists by saying that not even the *Iliad* can measure up to the extraordinary tale of cricket's Ashes legend. Certainly it cannot match up in terms of the massive breadth of a dazzlingly starry cast list, the huge range provided by its remarkable 123-year duration (and still counting), and the staggering depth and richness of a bewildering kaleidoscope of human emotion and achievement.

England and Australia have met each other 290 times on the fields of Ashes combat since what was almost a mythical birth of the competition for the tiny urn in the last four months of 1882 and the first weeks of 1883. Moreover, there have been 62 Ashes rubbers played and the present score reads: Australia 34 series wins, England 28. As the five 2005 Ashes Tests approach, it is Australia who currently hold the upper hand with a record of eight successive series victories behind them. Their modern-day champions, Glenn McGrath and Shane Warne, are still forces to be reckoned with, too, but Ashes history – like all the epic tales – will tell you that even the greatest of warriors falls in the end.

So while England awaits her new Achilles, a new Botham or a new Tyson or WG, all that is known to us watching mortals is that the great Ashes epic is destined still to go on even if such a figure does not emerge during this particular English summer. And, yes, for the assurance of long-suffering England followers, one day he will come . . .

In the meantime, I hope this book will further bring to life the long, complex, exciting and intriguing story of the Ashes.

There are dips into each and every one of the 62 individual Ashes series, and although the intention is to concentrate on some of the more curious, amusing or unknown aspects of the overall tale, the narrative keeps at least one eye on the central themes of Ashes glory and Ashes despair.

All the great cricketing heroes of England and Australia appear in these pages, too, along with mentions of many of their deeds. But for exhaustive accounts of every clash of bat and ball, the reader will have to refer elsewhere. This book in the main seeks, instead, to throw perhaps more light than is usual on some of the lesser characters that have found themselves caught up in the magnificent jousts between cricket's oldest rivals. There is fun and sadness, success and failure, and accident and happy coincidence to be found in the following pages. And through it all, hopefully, emerges a sort of alternative history of the Ashes – revealing, once more, its amazing grandeur of scope and content.

It remains only for me to thank Iain MacGregor, Jennifer Lansbury and Steve Gove, and all at Chrysalis and Robson Books, for their help with regards to the production of the book, and for their guidance and advice.

Many thanks are due, too, to Nasser Hussain for kindly agreeing to contribute a foreword. As he says, on behalf of England captains of more recent vintage, Ashes contests have not exactly been full of laughs for Englishmen during the past sixteen years. But, as Nasser also reminds us, incident of an unusual or amusing nature is never too far away when the Ashes are at stake.

Among my many sources of inspiration, which include Christopher Martin-Jenkins' excellent *World Cricketers*, I cannot allow that other true sporting epic – *Wisden*, in all its miraculous yearly forms – to get away without a sizeable mention and heartfelt thanks. Without its constant ability to keep me on the right path, my own journey would have come to a stumbling halt long before its end.

There are obviously many more strange and surprising stories surrounding the Ashes Tests which have not made these pages. But that, of course, is itself hardly strange or surprising – because the multi-layered story of the Ashes is a tale far too big for just one book.

Mark Baldwin
June 2005

1882–83

THE ASHES: CONCEIVED BY A PEN AND A FEMININE TOUCH

On the day that caused the Ashes to come into being, the excitement of the cricket was so great that one poor spectator died of heart failure. George Spendlove was his name, and he died at the age of 48, moments after Australia's second innings at the Oval on 29 August 1882 had ended on 122 – the highest total of the match – leaving England to make 85 for victory.

The unfortunate Mr Spendlove did not live to see the outcome, an Australian win by seven runs, but Fred Spofforth's second seven-wicket haul of the game and W G Grace's dismissal for 32 when he hit a drive straight to mid-off, contributed to such unbearable tension around the Kennington ground on that late Tuesday afternoon that another spectator reportedly bit through the handle of his rolled-up umbrella.

A full-strength England side, bowled out for 77, had lost for the first time on home soil to the Australians – and, a few days later, a mock obituary written by Reginald Brooks, a young London journalist, appeared in the *Sporting Times*. It read:

In affectionate remembrance of English cricket which died at The Oval, 29th August, 1882. Deeply lamented by a large circle of sorrowing friends and acquaintances, R.I.P. N.B. The body will be cremated and the Ashes taken to Australia.

They were words which took a hold in the popular public mind, and when the Honourable Ivo Bligh, who had already been invited by the Melbourne Cricket Club to take an England team out to tour Australia that coming winter, set out from Gravesend on the P & O liner *Peshawar* a fortnight later, he declared that he and his men would be trying with all their might to beat the Australians over three scheduled matches 'and bring back the Ashes'.

This he also announced as his objective when arriving in Melbourne, baffling Australians who had not the slightest knowledge of the *Sporting Times*' notice. Once explained to the hosts, the phrase nevertheless became part of the language surrounding the tour – and it was now that real-life romance gave precious new life to the Ashes concept.

Bligh and his men had landed in Australia on 10 November, after an eight-week sea voyage, and at a social event in the week before Christmas the England captain was introduced to Miss Florence Rose Morphy, of Beechworth, Victoria. Suffice to say that, by the time England came back from a 1–0 deficit to take the series 2–1, in front of huge crowds totalling more than 150,000 for the three matches, Miss Morphy and the Honourable Ivo had become quite attached to each other. Moreover, it was the lady, so history tells us, who got together with some of her girlfriends from Melbourne to present the dashing, winning English captain with a little urn to commemorate his side's triumphant reclamation of the symbolic prize.

Whether the ashes inside the urn are of a burned bail from the third match of 1882–83, which was staged in Sydney and won by England by 69 runs, or of a burned ball or even Miss Morphy's burned veil, is still a matter of conjecture and dispute. It is quite definitely an ashes urn, though, and the now fragile artefact – cricket's Holy Grail – has been on display in the MCC's cricket museum at Lord's since 1927. That was when the former Florence Morphy, by now Lady Darnley after Bligh had succeeded to the title of the eighth Lord Darnley in 1900, made a gift of the precious urn to MCC on the death of her beloved husband, whom she had married in February 1884.

There are a couple of curious postscripts, meanwhile, to the tale of the birth of the Ashes legend. First, the deciding third match, at the Sydney Cricket Ground, was played on two separate pitches – with each captain, Bligh and Australia's Billy Murdoch, having the choice of which strip they wanted to bat on in each innings.

And, when a fourth match (international games were not called Tests until the 1894–95 Ashes series) was suddenly added on to the itinerary – presumably due to the popularity and financial success of the three scheduled internationals – Australia won it by four wickets in a closely fought but experimental contest that used four different pitches for the four separate innings.

Thus, the very first Ashes 'series' ended as a 2–2 draw, but in historical fact it is England who became the first (and last) team to be able to travel homewards with the actual, original Ashes urn in their possession.

THE SAD TALE OF FRED MORLEY

Ashes history lacks for nothing in terms of courage and grit, but the performance in 1882–83 of Nottinghamshire's Fred Morley was a remarkable one nonetheless.

Morley, a left-arm seam bowler with a pleasing action and of remorseless accuracy, had played in the first Test ever staged on English soil, at the Oval on 6–8 September 1880. It was his first-innings 5 for 56, moreover, in an Australian slide to 149 all out, that was chiefly responsible for earning England a sizeable lead after W G Grace's debut 152 had taken England to a formidable 420. Following on, the Australians fought their way to 327 on the strength of Billy Murdoch's superb unbeaten 153, but Morley took another 3 for 90 and bowled 61 overs – almost twice as many as anyone else. England finally won the match by five wickets.

Morley, however, suffered a grievous injury in an accident which took place during the sea voyage to Australia in the autumn of 1882. After a two-day break in Colombo, the tour party's ship *Peshawar* made again for the open sea but was involved in a violent collision with another vessel, the *Glenroy*. Morley, thrown down by the impact of the collision, was knocked out and – it later transpired – suffered two fractured ribs.

Though badly hurt, Morley was by all accounts an uncomplaining soul and insisted on carrying on with the tour after receiving medical attention during the nine further days the *Peshawar* had to spend in Colombo for repairs. Nevertheless, he was unable to play in the opening Test of the 1882–83 series, which began in Melbourne two weeks after he had celebrated his 32nd birthday.

Brought in for the second Test, again in Melbourne, Morley went wicketless in England's series-levelling innings victory but bowled 23 first-innings overs at a cost of just thirteen runs. Then, in the decisive match at Sydney, he picked up 4 for 47 (from 34 four-ball overs) in Australia's first innings, and two important top-order wickets second time around. He and Dick Barlow, who grabbed 7 for 40 with his own left-arm medium pace, bowled unchanged for the 69.2 overs in which it took them to dismiss the Australians – who needed 153 to win – for a paltry 83.

Morley earned himself two more wickets in the hastily arranged fourth Test, taking his overall tally to sixteen in four matches at an average of 18.50 runs apiece; that, however, proved to be the end of his international career.

On his return from Australia he suffered a deterioration in his health, thought by many to be linked to the injuries and shock he had endured in the collision at sea. He died in September 1884, at the age of 33, from a condition described as 'congestion and dropsy'.

THE UNIQUE ACHIEVEMENT OF BILLY MIDWINTER

In the fourth Test of the 1882–83 series, a fine all-round cricketer named Billy Midwinter earned himself the unique achievement of being the only man to play for Australia, and England, and then Australia again!

After appearing for Australia against James Lillywhite's England team in both the first two Tests ever played, in 1876–77, Midwinter played four times for England on their 1881–82 tour of Australia. Within a year, however, he was starting a second 'career' as an Australian international cricketer by appearing in the first of his six Ashes contests.

Midwinter's incredible story began in the small Forest of Dean village of St Briavels, Gloucestershire, where he was born in 1851. Taken to Australia as a small boy by his emigrating parents, he was a good enough player to impress W G Grace when the great cricketer led a touring English side to Australia in 1873–74.

That led, in turn, to him being invited by Grace to play county cricket for Gloucestershire, because of his birth qualification. He played for the county from 1877 to 1882, thus becoming – in effect – the first overseas professional to appear in the domestic English game. His selection also provoked an extraordinary incident early in the summer of 1878 when he was contracted both for Gloucestershire and a touring Australian side.

When WG, to his considerable chagrin, turned up with his county team to play Surrey at the Oval and found that Midwinter was instead at Lord's, after being called there by the tourists to play against Middlesex, the good doctor pulled off what amounted to a cricketing kidnap. Grace jumped into a taxi cab and immediately made across London. When he reached Lord's he marched straight into the pavilion and hauled Midwinter out of the Australian dressing room. No doubt alluding, too, to the financial benefits, Grace reminded

Midwinter of the responsibilities that went with his county contract, and the player duly went straight to the Oval with WG. He also stayed away from the Australian team for the remainder of the summer!

Even in his Gloucestershire years, however, Midwinter continually commuted between English and Australian summers, returning to his home in Victoria. He was, at his best, a hard-hitting middle-order batsman, a steady medium-pace bowler and a fine fielder.

But Midwinter's amazing double (or should that be triple?) life ended in tragedy. When his wife and two children died, struck down by illness, he lost his mind and was confined to an asylum for the insane. There, on 3 December 1890, at the age of only 39, he too died.

1884

THE GLOVES COME OFF

England's retention of the Ashes in their first home defence came as a result of victory by an innings and five runs in the second Test of that summer's three-match series. It was also the first Test match ever played at Lord's, with England's fine performance under the captaincy of Lord Harris being spearheaded by the batsmanship of Allan Steel and the contrasting bowling styles of Ted Peate and George Ulyett.

Peate, a canny slow left-armer in an early manifestation of a Yorkshire tradition subsequently carried on by Peel, Rhodes and Verity, took 6 for 85 in Australia's first innings while his county team-mate Ulyett, a forceful fast bowling all-rounder in the mould that later produced Botham and Flintoff, took 7 for 36 to send the Aussies tumbling from 60 for 1 to 145 all out in their second innings.

Moreover, Ulyett's stock delivery – the banged-in off-cutter – forced Australian wicket-keeper Jack Blackham to retire hurt for 0 when the total was 94 for 6. Blackham had chosen to bat without gloves and his left hand was damaged when it was trapped between the sharply rising ball and the bat handle.

Steel's brilliant 148 was 110 runs more than England's next best score in their own first innings of 379, and another unusual occurrence accompanied his dismissal of Australia's first-innings top scorer 'Tup' Scott for 75. When W G Grace injured a finger in the field, it was his great friend and Australian captain Billy Murdoch who volunteered to act as a substitute fielder for England's champion. Murdoch, who had already fallen to Peate, thus became the first substitute fielder to take a catch in Test cricket when he caught out his own side's top scorer. Ironically, Murdoch later settled in England and, in 1891–92, actually played for England against South Africa in Cape Town.

THE GLOVES GO ON

W G Grace remains, 90 years after his death, one of the most instantly recognisable figures in cricket history. Grace, furthermore, was an all-round sportsman good enough when he possessed the lean physique of his youth to be a noted sprinter and hurdler. He is popularly remembered as the huge-girthed, long-bearded batsman who bestrode his generation and scored almost 55,000 first-class runs. It is not commonly appreciated however that, as a bowler, he also took an astonishing 2,876 first-class wickets with his round-arm, medium-pace leg-cutters . . . while it is certainly not widely known that he once took a catch keeping wicket in a Test match!

This incident occurred during the drawn third and final Test of the 1884 Ashes series, at the Oval, after Australia had gone past 500 with just six wickets of their first innings down. The Right Honourable Alfred Lyttelton, England's wicket-keeper and one of the great Renaissance men of his time, had already sent down a spell of lobs the previous evening, with Walter Read keeping wicket. Now it was decided that he should bowl a second spell – with his pads still on! Grace, meanwhile, who this time had taken Lyttelton's place behind the stumps, 'made a good leg-side catch to the first ball' (according to *The Times*) to dismiss Billy Midwinter.

Wicket-keeper and bowler celebrated by shaking hands in mid-pitch as the crowd cheered. Grace then stayed as keeper, wearing just the gloves, as Lyttelton proceeded to wrap up the Aussie innings for 551 by taking the last four wickets for just eight runs.

Lyttelton, who had been a member of the Cambridge University side which defeated the 1878 Australians, also played soccer for England and – as a professional lawyer – later held the post of Colonial Secretary in A J Balfour's Conservative Government between 1903 and 1905.

WG, who delighted in occasionally keeping wicket throughout his great career, is credited with five first-class stumpings besides his other, immortal, cricketing achievements.

1884–85

THE 'REFUSNIK' SERIES

England's 3–2 series success in Australia in 1884–85 is chiefly notable for the fact that the same XI played in all five Test matches. Such freedom from injury is almost unheard of in modern times, although it is still often the case that a winning team also happens to be a relatively unchanging one.

Another unusual feature of this rubber, however, is that it featured no less than three instances of players refusing to perform. To begin with, for the second Test at the Melbourne Cricket Ground, the Australian XI showed eleven changes after the whole team which had lost the opening Test refused to play unless they were given 50 per cent of the entire gate money. This demand was not granted, and no fewer than nine Australians thus made their Test debuts in a game which England unsurprisingly won quite comfortably by ten wickets.

With several of their first-choice players reinstated, however, Australia hit back in the third Test at Sydney to win a thrilling contest by six runs. England, chasing 214, were dismissed for 207 – the highest total of the match – despite reaching 194 for 6 following a stand of 102 between Wilfred Flowers and Maurice Read. But both were dismissed for 56 by 'The Demon', Fred Spofforth, who finished with 6 for 90 and a match analysis of 10 for 144.

England were left to reflect on the fact that Billy Barnes had not bowled a ball in the game on a pitch that seemed tailor-made for his style of bowling. Barnes, who had taken nine wickets in the previous Test with his accurate medium-pacers, was to finish with nineteen wickets in the series and was England's most successful bowler during the tour, but he reportedly refused to bowl in this game as a result of a quarrel with his captain, Arthur Shrewsbury.

Like many a cricketer of any era, Barnes also liked a drink and was once warned by his county, Nottinghamshire, not to keep arriving for matches in an inebriated state. He once made a match-saving hundred despite being the worse for wear and, on being reprimanded for his condition by the county committee, replied: 'How many of you gentlemen could make a hundred – drunk or sober?' On leaving the game in 1894 he became a pub landlord, but died only five years later at the age of 47.

The 1884–85 series was levelled at 2–2 when Australia, taking full advantage of their good fortune in the third Test, won the fourth game – also at Sydney – by eight wickets. Tensions were now clearly running high, and after tea on the third day one of the umpires – J H Hodges – refused to continue standing in the match due to the number of English complaints about his decision-making.

By this time, however, England were well on their way to a decisive innings and 98-run victory, with skipper Shrewsbury guiding his side to a first-innings lead of 223 by becoming the first England captain to score a Test match hundred, ending up on 105 not out. As a result of the umpire's withdrawal, the Australian all-rounder Tom Garrett, who had already been out twice, deputised for Hodges for the remainder of the match.

1886

GRACE AND GOOD FORTUNE

W G Grace's highest Test score was the 170 he made at the
Oval on 12 August 1886. It was an innings made out of 216
while he was at the crease, and set up an England victory by an
innings and 217 runs which enabled them to complete a 3–0
series whitewash. This Australian side was not as strong as
previous tour parties had been, and it was further handicapped
by the fitness struggles of Fred Spofforth, the fast bowler who
– more than anyone – troubled Grace with his pace and skill.

Spofforth, in fact, had once spreadeagled WG's stumps in
the nets when the future 'Demon' was an unknown eighteen-
year-old: the occasion was a practice session before a Boxing
Day fixture at the Melbourne Cricket Ground, during the
private 1873–74 tour to Australia organised by Grace. Now 30,
Spofforth was at the mature height of his considerable powers,
but an injury to his bowling hand early in the 1886 tour caused
him to miss a month's cricket and limited his effectiveness for
the rest of the trip.

WG came into the Oval Test with scores of just 8, 4 and 18
from the previous two matches, at Old Trafford and Lord's.
Understandably, then, he was uncharacteristically cautious at
the start of his innings, taking an almost unprecedented 130
minutes over his first fifty. By that stage, too, he had enjoyed
the first two of five 'lives': dropped at slip when on 6 and put
down by George Giffen off his own bowling at 23.

Grace, finally building up a head of steam, then raced to his
hundred in just a further 45 minutes – but, even so, was missed

12

at long-off when 60 and in the slips when 93. His fifth let-off came minutes before he was at last held at the wicket off the persevering but frustrated Spofforth. Yet, for all Grace's early scratchiness and good fortune, his innings was truly a marvel compared to that played by his opening partner, the left-handed Nottinghamshire batsman William Scotton.

Notorious for slow scoring, Scotton here took eighteen overs to get off the mark and, much later, remained on 24 for 67 minutes. When he was eventually bowled by Tom Garrett, whose eventual figures of 3 for 88 in an England first innings of 434 included a remarkable 55 maidens from 99 four-ball overs, Scotton's contribution to a first-wicket stand of 170 had been a mere 34.

The Times, mind you, reported his three-and-three-quarter-hour effort as 'a fine defensive innings'. That, perhaps, shows us how importantly an Ashes series was regarded even then!

1886-87

THE TEAM WHO WERE BOWLED OUT FOR 45 – AND WON!

Arthur Shrewsbury's 1886–87 England tourists – popularly known as 'Shaw's Team' after their manager, the great former bowler Alfred Shaw – won a truly sensational victory in the opening Test at Sydney after being bowled out on a difficult surface for a mere 45.

Percy McDonnell, the new Australian captain, was therefore perfectly justified in his decision, on winning the toss, to ask England to bat, thus becoming the first Test skipper to put the opposition in. Only George Lohmann, with 17 from number nine, made double figures and the total remains England's lowest in all Tests.

Yet England were not done. Bowling Australia out for 119, they reached a fighting 184 in their own second innings, with last pair Wilfred Flowers and wicket-keeper Mordecai Sherwin adding a crucial 31. Billy Barnes, with 6 for 28 from 46 four-ball overs, and Lohmann, who took 3 for 20 from 24, then proceeded to spearhead England's dramatic victory bid. Wickets fell at regular intervals as Australia inched towards their target of 111 – England's supposedly unlucky 'Nelson'.

At 61 for 5, and then 95 for 8, the game was continually in the balance. However, Lohmann then had Thomas Garrett caught for 10 and clean bowled Fred Spofforth for 5. Australia had lost their last two wickets for just two runs and were all out for 97.

1887–88

AUSTRALIA'S TURN TO GO LOW

It is not often that a team's star bowler has returned a match analysis of 88 overs, 50 maidens, just 87 runs, and 12 wickets (bowling four-ball overs of course) and still finished up on the losing side. But that is what happened to Charlie Turner, the legendary Australian fast bowler, when Walter Read's England side won the only Ashes Test of the 1887–88 southern hemisphere summer.

'Turner the Terror', as he was dubbed by cricket followers, had taken 6 for 15 on his Test debut just over a year earlier when England had been shot out for 45. Now, after his 5 for 44 from 50 overs had helped to reduce Read's England to 113 all out on the opening day, it was Australia's turn to hit a new low. Their 42 all out in reply, with just Tom Garrett (10) reaching double figures on a badly rain-affected pitch, remained their lowest total in all Tests until they were dismissed for 36 by England in 1902.

Again, Turner did his best to derail England, taking a second-innings 7 for 43 as the visitors were bowled out for 137. But the Australians hardly fared much better second time around against the slow left-arm spin of Bobby Peel and the masterful fast-medium of George Lohmann. The pair had shared all ten wickets in the Aussies' first-innings disintegration; now they shared a further nine as the home team slipped to 82 all out and defeat in such a low-scoring match by a whopping 126 runs.

1888

THE DOCTOR ADMINISTERS ASHES VICTORY

The 1888 Ashes series was chiefly notable for the elevation to the England captaincy, at the age of 40, of Dr W G Grace – and for the way he led his country to a 2–1 victory following the loss of the opening match.

Allan Steel had skippered in the first Test of the three-match series, which England had lost by 61 runs on a treacherously wet pitch, and Grace's second-innings 24 was the top score in a game in which Australia's 116 and 60 proved too much for England (bowled out by Turner and Ferris for 53 and 62). Steel, and three others, were dropped for the next Test at the Oval, and the England team was chosen by the Surrey home club's committee. Unsurprisingly, perhaps, there were five Surrey players in the selected XI.

Grace, opening up with Surrey captain John Shuter after Australia had been skittled for just 80 despite winning the toss, was dismissed by Turner for a single – but his England side did not fold at the sight of their champion's fall. Ulyett went too, for a duck, but from 6 for 2 England rallied through the Surrey trio of Shuter, Walter Read and Bobby Abel. The diminutive Abel, all five foot four of him, hit 70 and was joined by Billy Barnes (62) in a vital fifth-wicket partnership of 112. Then, after coming in at number ten, the powerful Lohmann struck ten fours in a Test-best 62 not out to boost England's total up to the riches of 317. Barnes was also a major force with the ball, taking 5 for 32 as the Aussies slumped in their second innings to 100 all out.

England, victors by an innings and 137 runs in front of more than 30,000 paying spectators over the two days of the game, now gathered themselves for the series decider at Old Trafford, which was due to start sixteen days later on 30 August. And what a strange deciding match it was.

Heavy rain before the match (it was in Manchester, after all) left the unprotected pitch soft and wet, putting a premium on winning the toss and electing to bat before a drying pitch made conditions unplayable. But WG did not fail, although England's supporters were understandably worried when Turner soon removed both Abel and Ulyett for ducks to leave the home side again 6 for 2. The Doctor, however, had the perfect prescription for the crisis: summoning all his experience and skill, he blunted the twin threat of Turner and Ferris to dominate a third-wicket stand of 52 with Read that was worth three times that in the conditions and wrested back the initiative for England. WG's 38 was one of his finest and most valuable innings, despite its comparatively small size in terms of runs scored – a fact soon underlined when it remained the highest individual score of the match. It also took a brilliant one-handed catch at long-on by the giant George Bonnor to dismiss England's captain, before solid middle and lower order contributions took the total up to 172.

With a hot sun drying out the pitch, a feared 'sticky dog' – the traditional term for a pitch which, in the days before covering, became badly affected by rain – was the result by the second morning. Good-length balls suddenly began to rear up at the batsmen after becoming 'stuck' in the surface, and Australia lost their last eighteen wickets before lunch – a record in Tests – to crash to 81 and 70 all out and defeat by an innings and 21 runs.

Grace, who many had thought had been denied the England captaincy up to this point because of the establishment's uncertainty about his abilities either socially or tactically (or both), was triumphant. He was to go on to lead England in four of their next five series as his colossal career moved into its fourth decade.

Australia, meanwhile, were left to reflect on being bowled out a second time in just 69 minutes – the match ending at

1.52 p.m. on the second day. Indeed, the shortest completed Test match in England had required only six hours and 34 minutes of playing time.

1890

ENGLAND PLAYERS PUT COUNTY BEFORE COUNTRY

How important, in a cricket career, is being selected to play for your country? A silly question, to modern ears, but in the 1890 Ashes series it was certainly not quite such a straightforward one. England, indeed, contested the pivotal second Test at the Oval that year without three of their leading players: Bobby Peel, George Ulyett and Andrew Stoddart.

The professionals Ulyett and Peel had both appeared in the first Test at Lord's several weeks earlier, respectively hitting a vital 74 and taking six wickets in a seven-wicket victory clinched on the final day by WG's magnificent unbeaten 75. Stoddart was one of the leading amateur batsmen of his generation, and a future England captain. Yorkshire, however, refused to release Peel and Ulyett for this match, on the grounds that they were required for the county's fixture against Middlesex at Bradford. Stoddart, who as an amateur could do as he chose, also opted to represent Middlesex in the same game rather than take on the Australians.

It was as well for England, then, especially with skipper Grace suffering a first-ball duck in the first innings, that Kent's left-arm seamer Fred Martin enjoyed an inspired debut. Nicknamed 'Nutty', Martin found Australia's batting easy to crack: he took 6 for 50 as they were dismissed for 92, and then another 6 for 52 as they slid to a second-innings 102 all out. England, after Grace had narrowly escaped a king pair when he was dropped at point off Hugh Trumble, squeaked home by two wickets to clinch the series.

It was tense by the end, though, and the winning run was an overthrow when John Barrett missed the stumps with England's ninth-wicket pair, the one-eyed fast bowler John Sharpe and the Scottish wicket-keeper Gregor MacGregor, both stranded in mid-pitch. All very strange indeed, but perhaps not as strange as the fact that match-winner Martin never played against Australia again and in fact earned just one more Test cap – against South Africa in Cape Town in March 1892.

1891–92

'WG' LOSES THE ASHES

The background to England's historic 1891–92 tour, when six-ball overs were bowled for the first time in Tests, is a fascinating one. Australian cricket was experiencing something of a slump in popularity, and two separate English touring teams in 1887–88 had incurred significant financial losses. The third Earl of Sheffield, however, was approached by Harry Boyle, the former Australian fast bowler who had managed the 1890 Australians in England, with a view to staging a further tour that would provide a timely boost to cricket Down Under.

Lord Sheffield needed little persuasion. A cricket-lover and philanthropist, he had entertained incoming Australian teams at his 5,000-acre estate in Sussex since 1884 and was as concerned about the future health of the game in Australia as he was at home. He immediately decided to donate £150, so that the Sheffield Shield trophy could be contested by Australian state teams, but also decided to support the proposed 1891–92 tour. Boyle, though, had insisted on one condition if England were to tour: the side must include W G Grace.

Despite the fact that he was well past his 43rd birthday by the time the tour began, and experiencing something of a slump in form, the great champion of English cricket was still by far the number one drawcard as far as spectators were concerned. Those in Australia, moreover, had not seen him since he played for his own private tour team back in 1873–74.

Lord Sheffield agreed to these conditions, and decided to accompany the England team and act as manager himself.

Grace was all for it, too, especially once he realised that the personal fee he had requested – a whopping £3,000, which would convert to well in excess of £100,000 in modern terms – was guaranteed. The size of the England captain's fee was the subject of much grumbling among the squad's seasoned professionals (Grace, after all, was technically an amateur!), but in public there were few moans. Everyone knew that the tour would stand or fall on WG's presence – and the good doctor was always more than aware of his own worth, and his enormous popularity and pulling power.

Just imagine, though, what today's television companies would have paid for exclusive rights to WG's first Ashes tour! As it turned out, the tour was a massive success from an Australian viewpoint, both on the field and in terms of the general good of cricket: crowds were sizeable and often huge, and the game did indeed receive the big boost that was intended. The England team's share of the gate receipts, meanwhile, came to more than £14,000, yet, without Lord Sheffield's benefaction, the tour would have brought a loss on the English side. It was estimated to have cost £16,000 to stage, including all wages and expenses, leaving Lord Sheffield to honour his promise to cover any losses out of his own pocket.

Grace himself said before the trip: 'I am anxious to go again, for I believe it will do the game good,' but it is doubtful whether he was quite so philosophical about it when England lost the first two Tests of the three-match series. In the end, in fact, the great man became quite grumpy. He hated losing, for a start, his opinion of local umpiring standards was low, and the verbal treatment he received from sections of the Australian public and press was similar to the sort dished out in later generations to the likes of Jardine, Larwood, Snow, Illingworth and Brearley.

Grace was genuinely shocked when Australia won the opening Test at Melbourne by 54 runs, despite his own scores of 50 and 25, and devastated when the second match at Sydney also went to the colonials. Yet the second Test featured one of the great fightbacks by a side severely depleted by injury and tragedy. Australia faced a first-innings deficit of 162, having been bowled out by George Lohmann (8 for 58) for 145, and then seeing Bobby Abel become the first England opener to carry his bat through a Test innings to finish on 132 out of a total of 307.

Australia, meanwhile, had lost top-order batsman Harry Moses to a leg injury which meant he could not bat in their second innings, and they were soon 1 for 1. Alick Bannerman, however, was then joined by the aggressive John ('J J') Lyons in a second-wicket stand which transformed the match. They added 174, with Lyons hitting 134 and Bannerman scoring a highly skilled 91 that had Grace himself saying that the Australian opener would be among his selections for a World XI.

The Australians, though by now building a decent lead, were dealt a further blow when fast bowler Charlie McLeod received a telegram from Melbourne informing him of the tragic death of his brother at the age of just 35. He only had time to bat up the order and score 18 (quite an achievement in the circumstances), before departing on the afternoon train to Melbourne.

But, even with their opponents now both a batsman and a bowler light, England could not recover. Australia's eventual second-innings total of 391 left England to score 230 for victory, but the inspirational all-rounder George Giffen took 6 for 72 and helped Charlie Turner ('The Terror') to bowl Australia to a 72-run success. Grace's dismissal, caught at the wicket slashing at Turner for 5, left England at 11 for 3 and with no way back. About the fall of Grace, the *Australasian* newspaper reported: 'The air was thick with hats, and rent with shouting. Such a scene has, perhaps, never been witnessed on the ground before as followed the downfall of the English captain.'

For consolation, WG was left only with England's thumping innings and 230-run win which followed in the relatively meaningless third Test at Adelaide . . . plus his tour fee, of course.

1893

QUITE A BENEFIT

Benefit matches still act as a popular and effective way of raising money for loyal cricketers in the English county game. Maurice Read, the professional Surrey batsman who had been an England regular for a decade, had a Test match granted to him as his benefit – and a decisive Ashes series match at that.

Read was not playing, having been dropped following two low scores in the drawn opening Test of the 1893 series at Lord's, but Surrey's committee decided that the second Test at the Oval was the perfect opportunity to reward his service to club and country. It was the first instance of such a gesture, and even the English weather was kind to Read: the match was played throughout in almost tropical heat. The 45-year-old W G Grace was back as captain after missing the Lord's Test through a finger injury, and he proceeded to win the toss and put on 151 for the first wicket with Andrew Stoddart, his deputy.

Australia's bowling attack was reportedly 'tight and hostile' despite the energy-sapping conditions, but Grace and Stoddart resolutely stuck to their task to score 68 and 83 respectively. The foundations for a match-winning first innings total had been laid, and the hard work of the two openers was not wasted as Arthur Shrewsbury (66), the debutant Albert Ward (55), the dashing Walter Read (52) and the precocious Cambridge University captain F S Jackson, with a brilliant 103 from number seven in just his second Test appearance, built England's total up to 483. Moreover, the twin threat of Turner and Trumble was neutered, as they each bowled 47 overs for just one wicket apiece, and only the combative George Giffen, who laboured through 54 five-ball overs for figures of 7 for 128, kept any sort of check on England's progress.

Australia, humbled for 91 in their first innings by the fast bowling of Bill Lockwood and the fluent left-arm spin of Johnny Briggs, fared much better after following on – but still lost by an innings and 43 runs. Lockwood, a rough diamond of a man, and Briggs, a much-loved, small and impish Lancastrian, took four and five wickets respectively for the second time in the match.

It was the decisive result in the series. The third Test at Old Trafford finished in a draw as England, despite a run-a-minute second innings opening stand of 78 between Grace and Stoddart, decided on the fall of the pair that at 1–0 up caution was the best policy and declined to continue the chase to score 198 in 135 minutes.

Read's Oval benefit, meanwhile, netted him £1,200 from gate receipts – a tidy sum – but a sad postscript to the tale of England's 1893 Ashes heroes is that three of the players who contributed so much to the Oval win met tragic and untimely deaths.

Stoddart and Shrewsbury both shot themselves, at the ages of 52 and 47, the former because of failing health and fortunes and the latter even more tragically after mistakenly believing he had contracted an incurable disease. The ebullient Briggs suffered an epileptic fit during the 1899 Ashes Test at Headingley, and the following year had a further breakdown. He died aged only 39 in an asylum in 1902. It is said that in the time he spent there before his death he would imagine himself bowling up and down the ward and, at the end of each day, would announce his bowling figures – with some pride – to the nurses.

1894–95

THE FIRST-BALL WICKET GLORY OF A
ONE-CAP WONDER

His son, who had the same name, became Sir Arthur Coningham and was an eminent air marshal in the Royal Air Force. Plain Arthur Coningham, however, born in Melbourne in 1863 and who died in a mental institution in Sydney a couple of months before the outbreak of the Second World War, was a more colourful character and a one-Test wonder with a unique claim to a place in cricket history.

Coningham, a fast bowling all-rounder, toured England with the 1893 Australians but did not play a Test. He made headlines for saving a boy from drowning in the Thames during that summer, an act of heroism that earned him a medal, but it was not until the second Test of the 1894–95 series – in his native Melbourne – that Coningham won his sole Australian cap. England had won the opening Test in Sydney, and were about to take a 2–0 lead at the Melbourne Cricket Ground, but not before Coningham enjoyed his moment of Ashes fame on the morning of 29 December.

When Australian captain George Giffen chose to bowl first, he tossed the new ball to the 31-year-old Coningham and asked him to send down the first over. Archie MacLaren, one of England's most celebrated batsmen of the era, was immediately dismissed by Coningham's very first ball – caught by Harry Trott – and Coningham ended up with 2 for 17 from eleven overs as England slumped to a paltry 75 all out. McLaren's dismissal, meanwhile, had provided the first instances in a Test of a wicket falling to the first ball of the match and to a bowler's first delivery at top level.

For Coningham to have performed this double feat in what was his only Test appearance is unique – but the match did not have a happy ending for him in more ways than one. Apart from the fact that he was dropped for the remaining two Tests of the series, after failing to take a wicket in England's second innings, he also ended up on the losing side.

Australia, themselves bowled out for only 123 in their own first innings, were then on the receiving end of a brilliant captain's innings by England skipper Andrew Stoddart, who also led his country in rugby union during a golden sporting career. Stoddart's 173 – the highest innings by an England captain until Mike Denness made 188, also at Melbourne, in the 1974–75 Ashes series – was supported by the first instance of all eleven players in a Test innings reaching double figures. Those scores ranged from last man Tom Richardson's 11 to Bobby Peel's 53, and England's great fightback total of 475 left Australia to score 428 for victory.

Coningham, batting at number nine, came in with hope all but extinguished at 254 for 7 and was soon bowled by Peel's left-arm spin for 3. Australia, eventually all out for 333, were beaten by 94 runs. They found defeat even harder to bear in that they had also lost the opening Test, by a margin of just ten runs, after totalling a seemingly impregnable 586 in their first innings and then forcing England to follow on. Coningham, meanwhile, had also been no-balled during England's second innings for throwing. A notoriously volatile man in temperament, he had deliberately thrown a delivery at Stoddart after becoming frustrated by the England captain's mastery.

A fine athlete, who also excelled at rowing, shooting, billiards and rugby, Coningham's first-class cricket career ended in 1898. Two years later, he became embroiled in a scandalous divorce case when he accused an eminent priest of being the third party in his wife's adultery. Coningham, moreover, chose to conduct the prosecution himself, but his efforts proved unsuccessful and the case was thrown out.

TROTT'S SCORCHING DEBUT

Ashes history is full of series that have burst into flaming life on the back of heroic individual performances, but rarely can anyone have provided such pyrotechnics in truly searing conditions as Australian all-rounder Albert Trott.

The younger brother of established Test player Harry Trott was still a month short of his 22nd birthday when he was selected to play against England at Adelaide in the third match of the 1894–95 series. Australia were by then 2–0 down, and the Ashes were slipping away. The heat was on, moreover, in more ways than one. Thermometer readings touched a reputed 155 degrees Fahrenheit in the open during the match, and the whole contest was fought out in blazing temperatures.

Trott, however, made scores of 38 and 72 not out from number ten in the order to inspire Australia to totals of 238 and 411; then, in England's second innings, he bowled his round-arm seamers virtually unchanged for 27 overs to take 8 for 43 and sweep his country to a 382-run victory. He also caught England's last man Tom Richardson, off George Giffen's bowling, to wrap up the win.

Incredibly, Trott was not required to bowl at all in the next Test – which Australia won by an innings and 147 runs on a dreadful batting pitch at Sydney – to level the series at 2–2. He still played his part, though, by coming in at number nine with Australia at 119 for 7 and bludgeoning his way to 85 not out. First he figured in an eighth-wicket stand of 112 with century-maker Harry Graham, and then he was joined in a further last-wicket partnership of 45 with Charlie Turner.

The final Test, at Melbourne, drew huge crowds and massive interest on both sides of the world; even Queen Victoria was reported to have asked to be kept abreast of the latest score, and the game was dubbed 'the match of the century'. Sadly for Trott, however, his own magic was spent. He scored just 10 and 0, and bowled 49 overs in the match for just one wicket.

In a wonderfully competitive affair, England emerged triumphant by six wickets, largely through the batting of century-makers Archie MacLaren and Jack Brown, the pace and stamina of Tom Richardson, and the all-round talents of Bobby Peel. Albert Ward also scored 93 in a match-winning third-wicket stand of 210 with the explosive Brown, who blasted his second-innings 140 at a run a minute and reached his first fifty in a record 28 minutes.

Yorkshireman Brown died tragically young at 35 with a brain disorder, but spare a thought too for the fate of the tall and muscular Trott. Omitted from Australia's 1896 tour of England, he never played for his native country again – although he did represent England in two Tests in South Africa in 1898–99 after forging a county career with Middlesex that was notable for a string of epic deeds with both bat and ball. Also, playing for MCC against the touring Australians of 1899, he achieved the still unique feat of hitting a ball (from the great off-spinning all-rounder Monty Noble) clean over the Lord's pavilion. When his first-class career ended in 1911 he became an umpire, but on 30 July 1914 he reacted to his rapidly failing health by shooting himself in the head at his lodgings in North London.

1896

PLAYERS TAKE STRIKE ACTION

With the 1896 Ashes series in the balance at 1–1, five of England's leading professional players threatened to take strike action and not to play in the deciding third Test at the Oval. The dispute was over match fees – fuelled by further resentment over what the professionals viewed as the preferential treatment of England captain W G Grace – and, in the end, two players actually sat out the Test in protest.

Grace's career had enjoyed a remarkable 'Indian summer' in 1895 when, before turning 47 in July, he had completed the epic double of becoming the first cricketer to score 100 first-class hundreds and to complete 1,000 first-class runs in May. His *annus mirabilis* continued in the same vein; a total of 2,346 runs in the season were plundered at an average of 51, including nine scores of 100 or more, and a national newspaper caught the mood of a country in awe of Grace's achievements by taking it upon itself to organise a special commemorative testimonial. The *Daily Telegraph* urged its readers to donate a shilling apiece to the great man, and soon the coins were flooding in.

Meanwhile, the MCC, who to the dismay of many cricketers had not organised such an initiative in the first place, were soon joining forces with the *Telegraph* – and Grace's county Gloucestershire also got in on the act with a similar appeal to its own members. Professional players around the country grew appreciably (and perhaps understandably) aggrieved when they saw huge amounts of cash being thrown at someone who, in theory, played cricket as an amateur and, as a practising doctor and already well off, clearly did not need the money.

WG's massive popularity, however, was such that the testimonial produced astonishing results. A total of £9,073 (plus eight shillings and threepence) was raised from the three sources – a sum worth more than £250,000 in today's money. Compared to the fee for playing a Test for England – then £10 – this was riches indeed; furthermore, during the next summer, the leading English professionals began to suspect that WG was receiving far more than £10 per game when he led the national team.

On the eve of the Oval Test five top players – Billy Gunn, George Lohmann, Tom Hayward, Bobby Abel and Tom Richardson – demanded £20 as their match fee, or they would refuse to play. Press reports confirmed that Grace's fees and expenses were the main source of their resentment. Four of the striking players were on Surrey's staff and the county club, as hosts the organisers of the Test, refused to meet these demands. On the morning of the match there was further drama when three of the Surrey players – Hayward, Abel and Richardson – backed down and were reinstated in the England team. But the two others, Nottinghamshire batsman Gunn and Surrey fast bowler Lohmann, carried out their threat.

England won the Test anyway, in a rain-affected, low-scoring contest in which Australia were dismissed for just 44 in their second innings, but the incident left a bitter taste for many years to come.

Grace himself was deeply angered by his team-mates' actions, feeling rightly that he had always gone out of his way to support benefit matches held for his professional colleagues and that the development of cricket as mass entertainment had been largely down to his own legendary deeds and status. The professionals, however, were also right to regard themselves as poorly rewarded and – try as they might – the need to balance the reality of WG's enormous contribution to the game with the staggering difference in their respective earnings from it was something they could never really come to terms with.

For Lohmann, meanwhile, the affair marked the end of the (statistically) greatest bowling career in Test history. The three wickets he had taken at Lord's in the first Test of the series meant that his eighteen-match England career had produced 112 wickets at an average of 10.75 – figures that make him both the bowler with the lowest average in Tests for all those taking 25 wickets or more and the most regular wicket-taker at a mere 34 balls per dismissal. Within five years, too, Lohmann was dead at the age of 36 after suffering from consumption.

THE BALL THAT SINGED THE DOCTOR'S BEARD

If there is a nineteenth-century equivalent to Shane Warne's 'ball of the century' to Mike Gatting in the 1993 Ashes series, it is the delivery from Ernest Jones that – so legend has it – passed clean through W G Grace's beard.

This iconic moment, for the whole of cricket as much as Ashes history, occurred on 22 June at Lord's – the opening day of the 1896 series. WG, a month short of his 48th birthday and still the England captain, was opening the innings with Andrew Stoddart on a pitch on which Australia had just been tumbled out for 53. Between them, Tom Richardson and George Lohmann had humbled the Australian batting, but the tourists still had the fearsome pace of Jones – a 27-year-old former miner on the first of his three Ashes tours to England. Short and stocky, he would sprint to the crease and hurl the ball down with all his might. He regularly achieved disconcerting bounce with this method and, when his career was finally done, more than one England batsman felt that Jones at his peak was the fastest and most awkward bowler they had ever faced on a Test match field.

Jones' opening ball to Grace, the first of the innings, was certainly one of the nastiest the Doctor ever faced. Exploding from just short of a length, it clipped the top of the bat handle and flew through the straggly edges of the most famous beard in the world. Still climbing, the ball shot over the head of James Kelly, the wicket-keeper, and flew away for four. To WG's exclamation, 'What d'you think you're at, Jonah?' the Australian paceman replied, memorably, 'Sorry, Doctor, she slipped!'

Grace, though shaken by the thunderbolt, was not about to give up his wicket lightly to the new tearaway. Gritting his teeth, he saw off Jones' opening burst and made 66 in front of 30,000 spectators to reach his 1,000 runs in Tests and set his England side on the way to an eventual six-wicket victory. 'The first ball I sent whizzing through his whiskers,' said Jones later, 'but after that he kept hitting me off his blinking ear-'ole for four.'

INDIAN GENIUS SETS ASHES ALIGHT

Only a story as epic and as rich as the Ashes could contain the tale of the first Indian to play Test cricket. What a tale, and what a player. Perhaps even the modern Indian batting greats, from Tendulkar to Dravid, from Gavaskar to Sehwag, do not possess the genius that illuminated the magical stroke-play of Kumar Shri Ranjitsinhji – later known as the Jam Saheb of Nawanagar, but referred to throughout cricket simply as 'Ranji'. His unique stroke, the leg glide, in which he deflected the full-length ball on his legs with his bat behind his front pad, has never been copied.

Born in 1872, in Sarodar, he came to England to study at Cambridge University. Widely known in his student days by the nickname 'Smith', he quickly announced himself as one of the greatest natural batsmen in the game's history. The future England captain F S Jackson, a Cambridge contemporary, soon awarded Ranji his cricket Blue.

Ranji made 77 and 150 on his county debut for Sussex, against MCC at Lord's, but his bow on the biggest stage of all was even more spectacular. Because Lord Harris, then president of MCC, raised objections to Ranji's selection, he had missed the opening Test of the 1896 series. But the Lancashire committee (each Test's host county chose the England team in those days) decided to pick him for the second Test at Old Trafford. Selected to bat at three behind Stoddart and Grace, he twice held England's batting together while scoring 62 and a brilliant unbeaten 154. Thus Ranji became only the second batsman after WG to score a century on his Test debut, and he was also the first player to hit a hundred before lunch in a Test – going from 41 to 154 on the third morning before England's second innings ended at 305 all out.

Ranji went on to appear in fifteen Tests for his adopted country, scoring 989 runs at 44.95, and he also hit 175 in his first Test in Australia on the 1897–98 tour, at Sydney.

His stroke-play was lordly and wristy, but his demeanour was far from haughty. By all accounts he was an approachable and friendly character, especially given his affluent and privileged background. But he also knew his own mind, and had strong views on the game. As a uniformed officer, he attended W G Grace's funeral in Elmers End, south London, in 1915 and after the First World War he served on the League of Nations. His nephew, K S Duleepsinhji, was similarly wristy and gifted and played twelve Tests for England between the wars.

1897–98

MCLEOD GETS HIS REVENGE

Charlie McLeod was a steady, reliable all-rounder from Victoria who differed from other Ashes cricketers in one major respect: he was deaf. He had made just one Test appearance for Australia before the 1897–98 Ashes series, but was to play a leading role as the Aussies wrenched back the urn that summer by an emphatic 4–1 margin.

England, however, won the opening Test of the series at Sydney – and, while doing so, dismissed McLeod in what can only be described as an opportunistic fashion. Australia had been forced to follow on when, despite an eighth-wicket stand of 90 between McLeod (who finished on 50 not out) and Hugh Trumble, they were bowled out for 237. Promoted from number nine to bat at three in the Australian second innings, the distinctly unflashy McLeod had reached 26 and helped opener Joe Darling to add 98 when, with the scoreboard at 135 for 1, he was bowled by a no ball. Not hearing the umpire's call on account of his deafness, he left his crease as if to make for the pavilion, and was run out by Bill Storer, the England wicket-keeper.

Darling went on to score 101, and the precociously talented 20-year-old Clem Hill made 96, but Australia's eventual 408 all out meant that England needed only 95 to go 1–0 up.

McLeod's own revenge, however, did not take long in coming. Asked to open when the second Test got under way in Melbourne a fortnight later, on New Year's Day, McLeod got his head down early on and later blossomed to hit 112, becoming the first Australian to score an Ashes century at the MCG. Australia's first-innings total of 520 was enough to produce an innings victory, and McLeod's second-innings haul of 5 for 65, from 48 overs, then helped to sweep England aside by an innings and thirteen runs in the third Test at the Adelaide Oval.

Nor was that the last of McLeod's contributions. In the fourth Test, back in Melbourne, he followed up the taking of two second-innings English wickets by scoring an unbeaten 64 – again as opener – to guide Australia to an eight-wicket win. And, in the fifth and final Test at the SCG, he top-scored in Australia's first innings with 64 in a closely fought contest that – due to Darling's rapid and historic second-innings 160 – ended up going the home side's way by six wickets.

Darling, indeed, became the first batsman to score three hundreds in a Test rubber and the first to aggregate more than 500 runs in a series. His third-Test 178 at Adelaide included a famous six-hit to reach three figures: it was the first time a player had gone to a hundred with a six, and indeed was the first time a six had ever been hit in a Test match without the aid of overthrows. In those days, remember, a six-hit had to deposit the ball clean out of the ground rather than merely over the boundary.

McLeod, meanwhile, finished the five-match series with 352 runs at an average of 58.66, and ten wickets at 23.60. The run-out incident had cost England dearly.

1899

WAS HE PUSHED, OR DID HE JUMP?

The 1899 Ashes series began with one of the most momentous occasions in cricketing history: W G Grace's last Test. Only, at the time, nobody knew that this would be his final appearance.

Australia arrived early that summer with their strongest squad since 1882, and England's challenge was to win back the Ashes. Change was afoot before the series began. For the first time, an England selection panel was formed, under the chairmanship of Lord Hawke, that would pick the national team for each of the five Tests in the series.

Up until then, there had only ever been three Tests per English summer – at Lord's, the Oval and Old Trafford – and it had always been the committees of the three host clubs, MCC, Surrey and Lancashire, that had chosen the England side for their particular match. In 1899, though, Trent Bridge in Nottingham and Headingley in Leeds were also included as venues for the five-match rubber, and Trent Bridge was to stage the keenly anticipated opener.

WG, as befitting the greatest name in English cricket, was asked to be a member of Hawke's newly formed selection committee – and soon he was reappointed to lead England in their first home Test since August 1896. It was Grace's twelfth Test as England captain and his 22nd overall. Each one had been against Australia, but now he was fast approaching his 51st birthday and many felt that Nottinghamshire's great hero, Arthur Shrewsbury, should have been given the honour of skippering England in their inaugural Test at Trent Bridge.

Shrewsbury, who was 44, did not even make the side because he was considered – like WG – far too immobile in the field. Billy Gunn, another legendary Nottinghamshire batsman, was however chosen at the age of 42 for his last Test appearance.

The old guard, though, were about to take their last bow. Symbolically, perhaps, WG opened the England batting with C B Fry, one of the exciting new breed of stroke-makers – and the pair added 75 for the first wicket after Australia had eked out a ponderous 252 in their own first innings. But Grace and Gunn both fell cheaply as the England second innings stumbled alarmingly to 19 for 4, before a lordly unbeaten 93 from Ranjitsinhji earned England the safety of a draw. And so, on 3 June 1899, W G Grace played his last scoring stroke for his country – a single off his old adversary Ernest Jones – before being bowled by a break-back from Bill Howell.

After the game, he reportedly told team-mate F S Jackson: 'It's no use, Jacker. I shan't play again.' But, when the England selectors met to pick the team for the second Test at Lord's, it appeared that Grace had still not made up his mind. Fry, who Grace himself had co-opted on to the selection panel, recalls in his autobiography how he turned up for the meeting at the Sports Club in St James's Square, London, several minutes late. As he walked into the room, WG said: 'Here's Charles. Now Charles, before you sit down, we want you to answer this question, yes or no. Do you think that Archie MacLaren ought to play in the next Test match?' Fry replied: 'Yes, I do,' prompting Grace to say: 'That settles it.' Fry's autobiography continues:

I sat down at the table. Then, and only then, did I discover that the question WG had asked me meant, 'Shall I, W G Grace, resign from the England eleven?' This had never occurred to me. I had merely thought it a question of Archie coming in instead of one of the other batsmen, perhaps myself. I explained this and tried to hedge, but the others had made up their minds that I was to be confronted with a sudden casting-vote. So there it was. I who owed my place in the England team to WG's belief in me as a batsman gave the casting-vote that ended WG's career of cricket for England.

It seems that WG, on this evidence, never actually tendered his resignation to the England selection panel, but merely allowed the case for his inclusion or exclusion to be debated in committee. Despite the intrigue, however, it does seem that Grace had genuinely come to the conclusion that it was time for him at last to leave the Test stage. Fry continued: 'Fortunately for my peace of mind, I found out afterwards that WG himself felt that he ought to retire, not because he could not bat or bowl to the value of his place, but because he could not move about in the field or run his runs.'

1901–02

BARNES MAGIC TRUMPED BY HILL

England had the better of the remainder of the 1899 series, but were frustrated by the weather at Leeds, rain washing out the third Test's final day when they required just another 158 for victory with all ten second-innings wickets intact. Australia then followed on at Old Trafford in the next Test, but MacLaren's team were in effect penalised by the law which at that time automatically imposed the follow-on for teams coming up 120 runs or more short of their opponent's total. England would not have opted to bowl again, given the choice, simply because it allowed Australia their best chance of escape against an already tired attack. This they duly did, and it was scant consolation for England, as Australia sailed home still as holders of the Ashes, that the law was duly changed as a result of this match.

When the teams met again, then, on England's 1901–02 tour, Australia were growing used to the feeling of having the Ashes. England captain MacLaren, meanwhile, was planning to unleash upon the Australians an unknown bowler by the name of Sydney Francis Barnes.

By then 28 years of age, and playing in the Lancashire League after an unsuccessful time at Warwickshire, Barnes had improved his method so much that he greatly impressed MacLaren when he faced him in the Old Trafford nets. The skipper immediately made sure Barnes was selected for the Ashes tour, and in his debut Test at Sydney he repaid MacLaren's faith by taking 5 for 65 as Australia were skittled for 168 in reply to England's first-innings 464. Barnes' fellow debutants, Len Braund and Colin Blythe, then shared nine wickets as the Aussies were dismissed for 172 second time around – and England's Ashes quest had begun magnificently.

Barnes followed up with match figures of 13 for 163 in the second Test at the Melbourne Cricket Ground, but even this was not enough as 25 wickets fell on a rain-affected pitch on the opening day and Australia rode out the storm with some superb batting from Clem Hill and Reggie Duff.

Australia had held back most of their leading batsmen in their second innings, to take advantage of improving conditions on the second morning, and Hill's 99 from number seven and Duff's 104 from number ten on his Test debut took the game away from England. Duff and future Australian captain Warwick Armstrong, himself having been dropped down to number eleven on his debut, even added a match-clinching 120 for the tenth wicket – the first three-figure last-wicket stand in Tests.

Even worse was to follow for England, bowled out for 175 to lose by 229 runs in Melbourne. After bowling just seven overs as Australia began their reply to England's first-innings 388 in the third Test at Adelaide, Barnes was unable to take any further part in the series because of a twisted knee. In his absence, Hill took command for Australia – adding, remarkably, innings of 98 and 97 in this match to his second-innings 99 at Melbourne. His sequence of scores in the 'nervous nineties' is unique, and he finished the series – which Australia went on to win 4–1 – as the first batsman to top 500 runs in a Test rubber without making a century.

1902

ENGLAND'S STRONGEST BATTING LINE-UP?

The team that represented England in the first Test of the 1902 Ashes series – and the first Test ever to be played at Edgbaston in Birmingham – is generally considered to be the strongest, batting-wise, in English cricket history. All eleven made first-class centuries during their careers, and Wilfred Rhodes – who had made his debut in W G Grace's last Test in 1899 and was still England's number eleven in this game – ended up opening the batting with the great Jack Hobbs!

The England XI, which totalled 376 for 9 declared before rain ruined the rest of the game (and caused Australia to be tumbled out for a mere 36 on a treacherous surface), went on to earn a combined 557 first-class hundreds. This figure is made up as follows: Archie MacLaren 47, C B Fry 94, Ranjitsinhji 72, F S Jackson 31, Johnny Tyldesley 86, Dick Lilley 16, George Hirst 60, Gilbert Jessop 53, Len Braund 25, Bill Lockwood 15, Wilfred Rhodes 58.

That Rhodes, the number eleven, made more first-class runs in his career (39,802) than anyone else in this team, shows that the depth of this particular batting order is impressive indeed. Yet, in terms of first-class hundreds and totals of runs made, the England teams of the 1920s were statistically way ahead. The team that contested the first Ashes Test of the 1928–29 series at Brisbane, for instance, went on to amass a total of 930 first-class hundreds. It was: Jack Hobbs 197, Herbert Sutcliffe 149, Phil Mead 153, Wally Hammond 167, Douglas Jardine 35, Patsy Hendren 170, Percy Chapman 27, Maurice Tate 23,

Harold Larwood 3, Jack White 6, George Duckworth 0. Hobbs, Sutcliffe, Mead, Hammond and Hendren alone plundered an extraordinary tally of almost 275,000 first-class runs between them in their respective careers.

SHEFFIELD'S MATCH

Great battles for the Ashes have been staged, more often than not, in stadiums and at venues almost as famous as the players themselves: Lord's, the cathedral of cricket, and the historic Kennington Oval; the vast bowl of the Melbourne Cricket Ground, and the atmospheric Sydney Cricket Ground.

But what about humble Bramall Lane? Yes, on 3–5 July 1902, the home of Sheffield United Football Club did indeed host an Ashes Test – and, more to the point, it was its only Test. Following the damp draws at Birmingham and Lord's, moreover, the Sheffield Test produced what proved to be the decisive result of the series, with Australia winning by the substantial margin of 143 runs.

Sydney Barnes, the great England bowler, initially found the Bramall Lane pitch to his liking, taking 6 for 49 as the Australians totalled only 194 in their first innings. Jack Saunders and Monty Noble then shared the ten England wickets, however, as the home side collapsed from 86 for 1 to 145 all out, and when Clem Hill compiled Sheffield's only Test hundred to build on Victor Trumper's whirlwind 62 in 50 minutes at the top of the order, Australia were in control of the match. Half-centuries from Gilbert Jessop and Archie MacLaren, the captain, were not enough to prevent Hugh Trumble and Noble, with a further 6 for 52, from bowling England out for 195 and Australia into a 1–0 series lead.

Yorkshire continued to play first-class cricket at Bramall Lane until 1973, but the ground never staged such a high-profile match again.

THE FATE OF POOR FRED TATE

The last two Tests of the 1902 Ashes series live on as being among the most exciting ever played. Australia won the fourth Test at Old Trafford by just three runs, clinching their retention of the Ashes in the process, before England gained some consolation at least with a thrilling one-wicket win in the final Test at the Oval that featured a 75-minute hundred by Gilbert Jessop and a nerve-tingling last-wicket stand between George Hirst and Wilfred Rhodes.

Jessop, dubbed 'The Croucher' for the way he hunched himself over his bat before jumping out to launch violent assaults on bowlers, came in with England at 48 for 5 in their second innings and still 215 runs away from their victory target. Jessop's counterattack, supported first by F S Jackson and then by Hirst, has gone down in cricket legend. After his spectacular hitting, however, came drama of a different kind. Hirst looked in control, after Jessop's exit for 104, but he lost both Bill Lockwood and Dick Lilley and – at 248 for 9 – England were still fifteen runs short.

Enter Rhodes, the number eleven destined to go on to become an England opening batsman. Reportedly telling each other that 'we can get 'em in singles', the two Yorkshiremen from Kirkheaton, who were to end up with a total of 118 first-class hundreds to their names, set out on their mission with grim determination and a coolness not apparent in an excited crowd. Hirst, who finished on 58 not out, always denied that he and Rhodes had ever spoken the famous words, but why spoil the story?

Yet, while Hirst and Rhodes could forever bask in the glory of a golden memory, poor Fred Tate of Sussex was left to reflect on the cards that fate had dealt him in the previous match at Old Trafford. It was his Test debut, and the match began on Tate's 35th birthday – 24 July. By then an extremely experienced cricketer, in the sixteenth of an eventual nineteen first-class seasons that were to bring him 1,331 wickets with his steady off-breaks, Tate could have been excused for seeing his Test call-up as a well-earned reward for so many years of honest toil at the county coalface.

And, at first, all went well. He could not take a first-innings wicket, but held a catch to give fast bowler Lockwood one of his six as Australia fell away from 256 for 4 to 299 all out. Then, at number eleven, he contributed 5 not out as England recovered from 44 for 5 to reach 262 on the back of a fine century from F S Jackson.

Australia's second innings, moreover, brought him two wickets for only seven runs, but by then things were beginning to go wrong for poor Tate. He dropped a straightforward catch to let off Joe Darling, Australia's captain and top scorer with 37, and Australia's partial recovery from 10 for 3 to 86 all out in worsening conditions left England to make 124 for the victory that would square the series at 1–1 and keep the Ashes alive with one match remaining.

Alas, when Tate came into bat as last man, England were 116 for 9 and needed him to stay with Wilfred Rhodes. But the Sussex man was bowled for 4 by Jack Saunders. England, bowled out for 120, had lost by three runs – the closest Ashes result in terms of runs margin, alongside England's three-run victory at Melbourne in 1982–83.

Tate, distraught at the end, was never picked for his country again – but said through his tears: 'I've a little lad at home who'll make up for this.' And indeed he did. Young Maurice, then seven, went on to take 155 wickets in 39 Tests and earn renown as one of England's greatest fast-medium bowlers. Thankfully, too, Fred lived until 1943 and so was able to witness his son's entire career and see his prophecy come true.

1903–04

ARNOLD'S EARLY STRIKE BEFORE FOSTER TIPS THE BALANCE

Ted Arnold, a Devon-born all-rounder whose ability with bat and ball helped his adopted county, Worcestershire, to win first-class status in 1899, struck the cricketing jackpot when he made his Test debut on 11 December 1903. It was in the opening moments of the 1903–04 Ashes series, in Sydney, and fast-medium bowler Arnold had Victor Trumper – then popularly recognised as the world's best batsman – caught by his fellow debutant and county colleague R E Foster with his very first ball.

As an omen, for both Arnold and Foster, it was especially apt: Arnold went on to take 4 for 76 in this innings and eighteen wickets in the series overall, while 'Tip' Foster scored the small matter of 287 on his own Test debut in this match. England, under 'Plum' Warner, went on to win the match by five wickets and – with further victories at Melbourne and Sydney in the second and fourth Tests – to snatch back the Ashes by a 3–2 series margin.

Arnold only played ten Tests in all, despite being good enough to score more than 15,000 first-class runs and take more than 1,000 wickets, and Reginald Erskine Foster won just eight caps. His epic 287, full of powerful boundaries, was his only Test century. His cricketing opportunities had already been affected by business interests before, in May 1914, he died at the age of 36 from diabetes.

Yet by then he had enjoyed a brilliant all-round sporting career At Oxford University he won blues for golf and rackets, as well as cricket and soccer, and he is the only man to have captained England at both cricket and soccer, gaining six caps as a footballer. Before the illness which was to cut short his life so tragically, Foster was already assured of his place among England's greatest games-players.

GOOGLY INVENTOR CLINCHES THE ASHES

Bernard James Tindal Bosanquet is famous for much more than being the father of the celebrated late ITN newsreader Reginald Bosanquet: indeed, as the inventor of the googly, his is one of the legendary names of cricket history. The Australians, moreover, were so stunned by Bosanquet's impact upon the 1903–04 Ashes series that they have ever since referred to the googly, or wrong'un, as the 'Bosie'.

It was the leg-breaks and googlies that Bosanquet employed in a spell of 5 for 12 at Sydney on 3 March 1904, that made sure England regained the Ashes. He took 6 for 51 overall in Australia's second innings of 171, to wrap up a 157-run win which clinched the series 3–1, and sixteen wickets in the four matches he appeared in during the rubber as a whole. He was not chosen for the second Test at Melbourne, where Wilfred Rhodes twice bowled Australia out single-handedly to take match figures of 15 for 124 despite having eight catches dropped off his bowling.

Bosanquet had made his Test debut alongside Arnold, R E Foster and medium-pacer Albert Relf in the opening Test of the series at Sydney, and was a tall figure who also often excelled as a stroke-making batsman. In 1908, he topped the national batting averages. Starting out as a fast-medium bowler, he found he could also spin the ball sharply. Experimenting with a tennis ball, often in a table-top game called 'twisty grab', he was three years into his 22-season first-class career when he first tried out his googly in a county match for Middlesex, against Leicestershire in 1900. Soon he was to become the first top-class practitioner of this difficult art, and his eventual haul of 629 first-class wickets came at the lowly cost of under 24 runs apiece.

Perhaps Bosanquet should have played more than just seven times for England; in the first Test of the following Ashes series, at Trent Bridge in 1905, his 8 for 107 swept England to victory by 213 runs. But, when he had Monty Noble stumped by Dick Lilley in the drawn third Test at Headingley, 35 days later, Bosanquet had taken his 25th and last wicket for his country.

1905

A TALE OF TWO CAPTAINS

Remarkably, the two opposing captains in the 1905 Ashes series – England's F S Jackson and Australia's Joe Darling – shared exactly the same birth date: 21 November 1870. Although they were exactly the same age, they did not share the same luck in this particular rubber, however; Darling called incorrectly at the toss of the coin in all five Tests, while Jackson not only won all the tosses but also led England to a 2–0 series win and headed both the batting and bowling averages!

His 492 runs came at 70.28, and included two brilliant centuries at Headingley and Old Trafford, while his thirteen wickets cost just 15.46 runs apiece. He also began the series by dismissing Darling for 0 in Australia's first innings at Trent Bridge. No wonder the summer of 1905 was called 'Jackson's Year'.

The son of Lord Allerton, the Honourable Francis Stanley Jackson was a tall and graceful batsman and a medium-pacer with a lovely action. He was later knighted and became a leading figure in politics, and always liked people to remember that Winston Churchill had been his fag at Harrow School. He first played for England in 1893, the year that he also led Cambridge to victory in the University Match. He saw war service in South Africa during the Boer War, but returned triumphantly to cricket in the 1902 Ashes series.

After a prolific Yorkshire career, he retired from cricket to serve as a Member of Parliament for a constituency in the county. He became, over time, a member of the Cabinet in Lord

Salisbury's second Conservative Government, Lieutenant-Colonel of the West Yorkshire Regiment, Governor of Bengal (narrowly escaping assassination), chairman of the Conservative Party, president of both MCC and Yorkshire, and chairman of the England selectors in 1934 and 1946.

As the son of a member of the Legislative Assembly of South Australia, Darling also became active in politics once his cricket career was over in 1907 (the same year that Jackson played his last first-class game). He became a member of the Legislative Assembly of Tasmania in 1921, helped to form the Country Party a year later and, in 1938, was awarded the CBE for public services. Despite the disappointment of the 1905 tour, Darling had already led Australia to three Ashes series wins. Neither he nor Jackson played another Test after the 1905 series.

WARREN'S MOMENT IN THE SUN

The one-cap wonder holds a bittersweet place in the annals of cricket history – sweet because at least they did realise the ambition of being chosen for their country, but so often bitter in that such a fleeting taste of the big time was by its nature almost bound to have ended in misery such as that suffered by Fred Tate. In more modern times, indeed, the tales of such men as Alan Butcher, Paul Parker, John Stephenson and Alan Wells feature more feelings of sadness and regret than joyous memory.

The story of Arnold Warren is, however, a strange one. Born in 1875 at Codnor Park in Derbyshire, Warren was a fastish right-arm bowler who could be said to have begun an honourable Derbyshire trade: he was the first in a long line of stout-hearted and talented seamers from the county to have been good enough to take more than 100 wickets in an English season. He achieved that milestone in 1904 and, in the following summer at the age of 30, he was called up to represent England in the third Test of the Ashes series, at Headingley.

F S Jackson's magnificent unbeaten 144 took England to 301 in their first innings, tailender Warren adding 19 with his captain for the ninth wicket before being run out for 7. Now, though, came the moment of truth for the new cap. Taking the new ball alongside George Hirst was a test of nerve on debut, especially against the aggressive and experienced opening pair of Victor Trumper and Reggie Duff. Yet Warren was more than equal to it, clean bowling the great Trumper for 8 to make the initial breakthrough and then, after Hirst had sent back Clem Hill, having Monty Noble caught by Tom Hayward.

Australia rallied from 36 for 3 through Duff and Warwick Armstrong, but Warren returned to dismiss the giant Armstrong for 66 before also grabbing the wicket of Aussie skipper Joe Darling for just 5. Finally, Warren was brought back again to bowl last man Frank Laver and, with Australia all out for 195, earn himself the superb analysis of 5 for 57.

More, however, was to come. Even though the match ended as a draw, with Australia holding on gamely at 224 for 7, Warren had the ecstatic experience of grabbing Trumper's wicket for a second time – and for a duck, no less. He could not manage another wicket, in 20 overs that cost 56 runs, but match figures of 6 for 113 were still something to be proud of on Test debut.

What happened next? England called up the 29-year-old Lancastrian pace bowler Walter Brearley in Warren's place, to bowl on his home ground of Old Trafford, and Brearley took four wickets in each Australian innings as the Ashes were clinched by England's innings and 80-run victory in that fourth Test. Warren, with a Test bowling average of 18.83, was never called upon by his country again.

1907–08

SPARE GUNN COMES TO ENGLAND'S RESCUE

Being in the right place at the right time is often the key to a successful sporting life, and for Nottinghamshire's George Gunn that was certainly true of his international career. Gunn, whose uncle William and elder brother John also played Test cricket for England, had begun his own first-class career in 1902 and soon made an impression with his often unorthodox approach to batting. He was essentially a sound technician, and could play accordingly, but often he would do something outrageous – mainly because he had the reflexes and talent to do so. When the mood took him, he would walk away outside his leg stump to cut a ball square on the off side, or go down the pitch to fast bowlers. Small and wiry, he also however suffered from health problems and in the English winter of 1907–08 decided to travel to Australia to benefit from the warm weather.

When Arthur Jones, the England captain and a fellow Nottinghamshire player, fell seriously ill and needed hospital treatment in Brisbane, Gunn was summoned to join the MCC party. For the first Test against the Australians, at Sydney, the 28-year-old was then selected – ahead of a young Jack Hobbs – to bat at number three. Marching in when acting captain Frederick Fane was dismissed for just 2, Gunn responded by scoring 119 out of an England total of 273. He also top-scored with 74 in the England second innings, although Australia emerged from a fiercely fought contest with a thrilling two-wicket win.

Gunn then held his place throughout the five-match Ashes series, scoring 65 at Adelaide and 122 not out in the final Test back at Sydney, and he finished up heading the England batting averages with 51.33. He and Hobbs (who had made 83 on his own Test debut in the second match of the series at Melbourne – another exciting game which England won by one wicket) opened England's innings together in the fourth Test, and added 134 for the second wicket in the first innings of the final Test.

Australia won the series 4–1, deservedly so despite the closeness of the early exchanges, but Gunn had seized his chance to add a further chapter to his famous family's list of cricketing achievements – his uncle Billy having also by now founded his bat-making business Gunn & Moore. George Gunn went on to play fifteen Tests, and was chosen as an original member of the 1911–12 tour to Australia – where he was again a highly consistent performer at number three and averaged 42.33 in the five-match rubber.

There is also an unusual postscript to Gunn's career. Remarkably, his last four Test appearances came in the West Indies in 1929–30, when he was well over 50 and had been recalled to international duty after a record interval of seventeen years and 316 days.

HEROICS FROM HILL AND HARTIGAN

The 1907–08 series swung on the result of the third Test at Adelaide, and it was won for Australia largely through a remarkable eighth-wicket stand of 243 between Roger Hartigan and Clem Hill.

Australia were only 102 runs in front at 180 for 7 in their second innings when an unwell Hill came in at number nine to join Hartigan, who was making his Test debut. Hartigan, a stylish batsman given his Test chance at the age of 27, had already shown up well in the Australian first innings when he scored 48, but this was altogether a different proposition. The English bowling attack comprised Sydney Barnes, Wilfred Rhodes, Len Braund, Arthur Fielder and Jack Crawford, and the tall, cadaverous-looking Barnes had already clean bowled both Victor Trumper and Charlie Macartney in this innings.

But Hill, who had been unable to field because of influenza, dug in determinedly and his solid presence gave Hartigan confidence that the pair could save the game. Slowly, in sweltering conditions, they began to gain the upper hand against England's tiring bowlers. Eventually, Hartigan fell to Barnes for 116, but Hill's brave innings continued until he had reached 160. Australia, who thanks to their eighth-wicket pair had managed to total 506, then dismissed England second time around for 183. Jack O'Connor, like Hartigan making his debut, shared the ten English wickets with Jack Saunders and Australia's final winning margin was a decisive 245 runs.

Hartigan also played in the Australian 49-run win in the fifth and final Test in Sydney – scoring 1 and 5 – but that proved to be the end of his international career, as he did not play in any of the Tests after being selected for the 1909 Ashes tour.

1909

WHEN ENGLAND'S SELECTORS 'TOUCHED THE CONFINES OF LUNACY'

No fewer than 25 players were summoned from the shires to represent England in the five-match 1909 Ashes series and, unsurprisingly, England lost the rubber 2–1. Yet amid the often bewildering comings and goings (for instance, H A Gilbert was in the fifteen selected for the first Test at Edgbaston, but omitted from the eventual XI and never chosen again) there were some personal moments of glory.

Take Albert Relf. He had already toured Australia and South Africa with England, and was also destined to win the last five of his thirteen Test caps on the 1913–14 tour to South Africa, but the second Test in 1909 was his only international appearance on home soil. Relf had been one of the four players omitted at Edgbaston, but the England selectors made five changes (he, Tom Hayward, George Gunn, John King and Nigel Haigh replaced C B Fry, Gilbert Jessop, Wilfred Rhodes, George Thompson and Colin Blythe) despite seeing their team thrash the Aussies by ten wickets in the opening Test. King, Leicestershire's 38-year-old all-rounder playing in his only Test, top-scored with 60 in England's first innings and then found himself opening the bowling with his left-arm spin.

Relf came on first change, and his medium pace brought him 5 for 85 from 45 overs as Australia won a first-innings lead of 81 that was almost entirely due to an unbeaten 143 from Vernon Ransford. On a pitch becoming difficult to bat on, it was the decisive innings and Ransford also benefited from being dropped three times – twice off King. England's subsequent collapse to 121 all out in their second innings left Australia with a simple victory target, although Relf had the dangerous Warren Bardsley caught at the wicket for 0 before they levelled the series 1–1.

Six wickets at a cost of 94 runs, however, were not enough to keep Relf in the team – and England's selectors jettisoned him, Hayward, Gunn, King, Arthur Jones and Haigh as they again went in for wholesale changes. To no avail, either, as Australia won the third Test at Headingley by 126 runs to retain the Ashes. Even Jack Hobbs did not survive the chop for the fourth Test and – after that and the final match at the Oval had been drawn – only Archie MacLaren, the captain, and wicket-keeper Dick Lilley remained as England ever-presents in the series.

The Oval Test, meanwhile, produced the strange case of Douglas Ward Carr, a club bowler from Maidstone in Kent plucked seemingly out of the air by the selectors in one last, desperate throw to get something out of the series. Indeed, the choice of Carr, allied to the dropping of George Hirst and especially the failure to pick any out-and-out pace bowler, prompted the normally reserved *Wisden* to report that the England selectors had 'touched the confines of lunacy' with their choice of bowling attack on a typically firm and fast Oval pitch.

Carr's elevation was extraordinary: first, he was 37, and second, he had only begun playing first-class cricket earlier that summer when Kent called him up for a match against Oxford University. Until the age of 32 he had simply bowled leg-breaks in club cricket, but then he began to practise the googly and, a year later, he 'lost' his stock leg-spinner. Forced, in effect, to depend almost exclusively on the googly, he found that he had greater and greater success. After his county came calling, he found himself selected for two Gentlemen v Players games during 1909 – and proceeded to take fifteen wickets in those matches. He also picked up 51 scalps in seven County Championship outings – and suddenly found himself the 25th man thrust into England duty in an Ashes series that had started so brightly but had now gone so wrong.

In that era, it was often the case that teams would open up with a fast bowler at one end and a spinner or medium-paced cutter from the other. In many cases, the two bowlers, of whatever sort, considered best would open up and do the bulk of the bowling. Thus it was that, when Australia won the toss at the Oval on 9 August, Carr found himself bowling the first over of the match and sharing the new ball with Sydney Barnes. And, moreover, after seven overs he had figures of 3 for 19. Syd Gregory, bowled, and Monty Noble and Warwick Armstrong, both lbw, were his distinguished victims. When Barnes bowled Vernon Ransford for 3, Australia were 58 for 4 on a fine batting track and the England selectors were at last expecting some compliments.

Carr, however, then began to be overbowled by MacLaren and Australia counterattacked brilliantly through the stroke-play of Warren Bardsley, who made 136, Victor Trumper (73) and Charlie Macartney (50). Carr did later pick up two tail-end wickets, but his five wickets in 34 overs eventually cost 146 runs.

He and Barnes also did the bulk of the bowling in the second innings but, whereas Barnes took 2 for 61 from his 27 overs, Carr's 35 overs cost a further 136 as Bardsley plundered his second hundred of the match. He did, though, ensnare Armstrong for the second time and also had Trumper stumped just before an Australian declaration left England with no option but to bat out time for a draw. Carr's match analysis was 7 for 282 from 69 overs – not memorable when looked at coldly, but in the circumstances more than a decent effort against one of the most powerful batting line-ups that Test cricket has seen.

It was Carr's only Test appearance, and it coincided with the modest England debut (he scored just 8 and took no wickets) of a far more famous man of Kent – Frank Woolley. But the Ashes story is all the richer for the tale of Carr, the club bowler who rose from obscurity to perform so creditably on cricket's biggest stage.

1911–12

THE STAND-IN SKIPPER WHO WON BACK THE ASHES

John William Henry Tyler (Johnny) Douglas is the only Ashes-winning captain who has been lost at sea.

His tragic death, at the age of 48, was also an heroic one: he drowned in waters off Denmark as he tried to save the life of his father after the ship on which they were travelling collided with another in fog seven miles south of the Laeso Trindel lightship. Yet Douglas should not have been England's leader at all for the triumphant 1911–12 Ashes campaign, when they overturned a 1–0 deficit to emerge as 4–1 series winners.

First, it was C B Fry who was offered the captaincy as the MCC pondered on who best to entrust with the mission of recovering the Ashes following the disappointments of 1907–08 and 1909. Fry, however, declined the honour, citing the need to continue his zealous work with new recruits on the training ship *Mercury*, which was based on the River Hamble. In his place, the tour captaincy went to Pelham ('Plum') Warner and, initially, Essex skipper Douglas was merely required to offer advice in his capacity (along with Frank Foster of Warwickshire) as a current county captain.

Warner's tour started well, as he hit 151 against South Australia at Adelaide, but soon afterwards he was taken seriously ill and was sent to a nursing home to recuperate. From there, after he realised he would be able to take no further part in the tour as a player, Warner decreed that Douglas should take over as, at 29, he was seven years the senior. Yet both all-rounders, Douglas and Foster, had played no Test cricket before this tour; indeed, they were among the five debutants selected in the England team which started the series at Sydney.

This first Test did not go well for England, who lost by 146 runs. And, to make matters worse, Douglas riled his star bowler, the testy and temperamental Sydney Barnes, by taking the new ball himself alongside Foster. In the opening tour match at Adelaide, Warner had opened the bowling with Foster and Barnes – but Douglas, on assuming command, had given himself the new-ball role ahead of Barnes in the other warm-up matches against New South Wales and Queensland. Eye-witnesses said that Barnes flew into a terrible rage as Douglas prepared to bowl the second over of the first Test; Jack Hobbs and Frank Woolley both tried to placate him, but Barnes took it as a personal slight not to be given the opportunity to operate with the new ball. In the end, Barnes bowled 65 overs in the match – taking 3 for 107 from 35 overs in the first innings – but Trumper made 113 and Roy Minnett 90 in his first Test innings, and Australia were always in command of a match that, being the series decider, went into a sixth day.

With shades of the impact that another unorthodox Australian spinner was to make upon the Ashes story in the last decade of the twentieth century, the magical googly bowler Herbert Hordern marked his first Test against England by taking 7 for 90 in the second innings and 12 for 175 overall. Hordern was as dark in complexion as Shane Warne's features are sunny, but his work as a doctor prevented him from representing Australia in England, and from playing much international cricket. Nicknamed 'Ranji' because of his alleged likeness to England's great Indian batsman, he took 46 wickets in his seven Tests, and 32 of them in this series at an average of 24.

That England could still emerge as overwhelming winners of the series, given Hordern's performance and the fact that the Australian batting was of such considerable strength, is in no small part down to what happened immediately after the opening Test. Warner, still on his sick bed, summoned Douglas for a chat – and the main subject of their conversation was the treatment of Barnes. When the second Test began, at the MCG, nine days after the Sydney match had ended, and when Australian captain Clem Hill again won the toss and decided to bat first, it was Foster and Barnes who this time took the new ball.

It was also the turning point of the entire series. Foster delivered the first over, a maiden. Then Barnes, who had felt unwell on the morning of the match but insisted on playing, bowled Warren Bardsley off his pads with his very first ball. He gave a meaningful look in the direction of his captain.

Next, two overs later, the tough opener Charles Kelleway was lbw to an inswinger that straightened. Hill was castled by a beautiful, spiteful ball that swung in and cut away to clip the top of his off stump and, soon after, Warwick Armstrong snicked to 'Tiger' Smith, England's debutant wicket-keeper, who was standing up to the stumps.

Barnes had taken four wickets for one run in five overs, and Australia were 14 for 4 when a brief shower of rain drove the players from the field. When they returned, however, the tempest that was Barnes had still not blown itself out. After Foster had bowled Trumper for 13, Barnes had Rob Minnett caught by Hobbs for 2. Australia went into lunch at 38 for 6, and in a state of shock; Barnes had figures of 11–7–6–5, and the debate about who should propel England's precious new ball had been settled.

Although they rallied somewhat to reach 184 (Barnes finishing with 5 for 44), Australia found themselves behind in the game once the 20-year-old Jack Hearne, in his second Test, had scored a maiden century and added 127 for the second wicket with Wilfred Rhodes. Barnes then took three more second-innings wickets, this time in a supporting role for his new-ball partner Foster, whose whippy left-arm seamers earned him 6 for 91, and England needed only 219 to win.

Hobbs and Rhodes opened up with a stand of 57, and then the masterful Hobbs was joined by George Gunn in a further partnership worth 112 before going on to 126 not out in 227 minutes. It was the first of the great man's twelve centuries against Australia, and England's eight-wicket win – inspired as it was at the dramatic outset by Barnes – had pulled them level at 1–1.

The momentum was now with England, and Barnes picked up five-wicket hauls in each of the next two Tests while Hobbs hit 187 in the third Test at Adelaide – where England won by seven wickets – before being joined by Rhodes in an epic opening partnership of 323 in the fourth Test back in Melbourne. On that famous occasion Hobbs made 178 and Rhodes 179, setting up England's Ashes-clinching victory.

Fittingly, perhaps, it fell to stand-in skipper Douglas to wrap up the glorious innings and 225-run win. After Foster and Barnes had both struck with the new ball – they were to take 32 and 34 wickets respectively in the series – Douglas brought himself on to deal with the Australian middle and late order. This he did to great effect, ending up with his best Test figures of 5 for 46 when he claimed the wicket which confirmed the regaining of the Ashes.

1912

WHEN THE ASHES BECAME PART OF A THREE-WAY TUSSLE

England's wet summer of 1912 was the only time that an Ashes series has been played out within the format of a separate tournament. A brainchild of Sir Abe Bailey, the Triangular Tournament of 1912 consisted of England, Australia and South Africa playing each other three times. It has never been repeated.

Three of the nine matches were ruined by the weather, however, and the comparative weakness of the South Africans meant that they were defeated five times out of six. Their single draw was mainly as a result of rain which caused the abandonment of their third Test against Australia, although they had managed to gain their only first-innings lead of the tournament before the bad weather had the final say. In the end, England's first two meetings with Australia having resulted in rain-afflicted draws at Lord's and Old Trafford, the final Test between the two countries at the Oval in late August was going to decide the outcome both of the Ashes contest and the tournament itself.

Although at this stage the Australians had only gained two wins against South Africa to England's three, the tournament organisers decreed that the victors of what was to be the first 'timeless' Test to be staged on English soil would be crowned as the champions of the event. This certainly concentrated the minds of Jack Hobbs and Wilfred Rhodes, by now England's established opening pair, who immediately put on 107 on the first morning. It proved to be the highest partnership of the match, as conditions quickly deteriorated and the surface became more and more spin-friendly.

Frank Woolley's 62 had enabled England to reach 245 in their first innings, and now Australia were skittled for 111 in reply with Woolley's slow left-arm reaping 5 for 29 in support of the saturnine, miserly and tireless Sydney Barnes whose 27 overs and 15 maidens brought him figures of 5 for 30. England's position was further strengthened when C B Fry, who had this time accepted MCC's offer to captain his country for the summer, hit a brilliant 79 full of breathtaking drives to prevent a batting slide against the spitting turn being achieved by Gerry Hazlitt, the medium-paced off-break bowler who was to die tragically young of a heart attack three years later at the age of 27.

Hazlitt's 7 for 25 from 21.4 overs could not halt England's progress to 175 and, against the left-armers Harry Dean and Woolley, Australia had no chance of reaching their win target of 310. Lancashire's Dean, in his third and final Test, picked up 4 for 19 while Woolley bagged his second five-wicket haul of the game (5 for 20) as Australia plummeted to 65 all out.

1920–21

THE GIANT WHO DEFIED MALARIA ON HIS WAY INTO ASHES LEGEND

In the immediate aftermath of the Great War, English cricket seemed denuded of bright bowling talents. Gone, either into international retirement or into the mud of the Flanders fields, were the likes of Barnes and Blythe, cut down at Passchendaele, Braund, Hirst, Brearley, Crawford and the dashing, fast-bowling Major William Booth of Yorkshire, who fell on the Somme. There was still Woolley and Rhodes to bowl their left-arm spin, steadily if not spectacularly, but the England party which left to defend the Ashes in 1920–21 had no cutting edge to speak of – and was subsequently exposed as such.

Australia, meanwhile, were about to set sail into a golden age of their own – led by the man who was to win eight of the ten Tests in which he captained his country against England.

Warwick Windridge Armstrong was not known as 'The Big Ship' for nothing. Six foot two and slim when he first played Test cricket in 1901–02, he had bulked up à la W G Grace by the time the 1920–21 Ashes series came around. Not even Grace, though, ever tipped the scales at as much as 22 stone, but this was Armstrong's fighting weight in his two triumphant Ashes-winning campaigns. And, despite his 40-plus age and excess poundage, Armstrong was still very much a fighting force.

In the 1920–21 campaign, in particular, he was a major player for a side which collectively scored ten hundreds, as well as being a tough and strong-willed leader. He also took nine wickets, to provide excellent support in an attack led by the pace of Jack Gregory (23 wickets) and based around the spin of

Arthur Mailey, who took 36 wickets in the four Tests in which he bowled.

Armstrong's performance in the fourth Test at Melbourne sums up the big man as well as anything. He had already scored 158 in the opening match at Sydney, and another 121 in the previous Test in Adelaide, in a victory that swept Australia into a 3–0, Ashes-regaining lead, but three weeks later Armstrong was feeling weak from an attack of malaria.

So what did he do? Well, he only bowled five overs in the game, compared to the 90 he had sent down in the first three Tests, but he also strode in with Australia at 153 for 5 in reply to England's first-innings 284, initially added 145 for the sixth wicket with Jack Gregory and went on to finish up unbeaten on 123. It was his fourth and last hundred against England, and his sixth in all Tests, and it enabled Australia to gain a lead of 105. This, in turn, gave Mailey the opportunity to tempt and tease England's batsmen with his infinite varieties of leg-breaks, top-spinners and googlies and – eventually – to end up with the remarkable figures of 9 for 121 from 47 overs. England, bowled out for 315 second time around, ended up losing by eight wickets and were another step on the way to a 5–0 series humiliation.

Armstrong's glory was complete, and not even illness could stand in his way. Legend has it that he downed a couple of large whiskies to help him through the malaria attack. Whatever, in 1920–21 England were crushed beneath an Australian juggernaut, driven by a one-man dump-truck.

IF YOU BLINKED, YOU'D HAVE MISSED IT

Amid all the remorseless Australian success of the 1920–21 Ashes series there was one very sad tale to tell on the Aussie side of things. Blink, and you would have missed Roy Park's Test career.

His wife, in fact, did almost that. Sitting in the stands of the Melbourne Cricket Ground on New Year's Eve, 1920, she is reported to have bent down to pick up her knitting just at the moment her husband was missing the only ball he ever received in Test cricket. Coming in at number three following an opening partnership of 116 between Warren Bardsley and the departing batsman, Herbie Collins, Park was immediately clean bowled by England fast bowler Harry Howell.

Australia won this second Test of the series by an innings and 91 runs, but that was no consolation to Park, then 28 and a batsman who would surely have played more times for his country in earlier years but for the First World War. Later, his medical duties as a doctor also militated against his cricket, but in the previous Australian domestic season of 1919–20 he had averaged 83.71 for Victoria in the Sheffield Shield, including a career-best score of 228 against South Australia.

His only other contribution to his sole Test match, however, was to bowl a single over during England's first innings, at a cost of nine runs. Test cricket can be the cruellest of games, as Dr Roy Park would no doubt have told you.

HARRY'S GAME

England in 1920–21 were buried beneath an avalanche of Australian runs. In the series the Aussies ran up successive totals of 267, 581, 499, 354, 582, 389, 211 for 2, 392 and 93 for 1. Johnny Douglas, England's captain, just did not have the bowling resources available to him in his previous, successful, Ashes tour of 1911–12. Percy Fender and Cecil Parkin took 28 wickets between them at a cost of 38 runs apiece; the rest of the bowlers a total of 37 at 59.

But at least England's batting had its moments, with Jack Hobbs scoring two hundreds and Charles Russell and Harry Makepeace one each. Makepeace's 117, in the fourth Test at Melbourne, was of particular merit in that – at 39 years and 173 days of age – he became the oldest player to score a maiden Test hundred.

Yet even getting on the tour in the first place had been an achievement for the previously uncapped Lancashire batsman, who had begun his first-class career back in 1906 and had made his name as a predominantly defensive player. Makepeace had also played four times for England at football, becoming the seventh member of an exclusive club of just twelve men to have represented England at both cricket and soccer, and with Everton he won an FA Cup winners' medal. The four Test appearances he made in this series added up to his lot in international cricket, but he also scored 60 and 30 in England's third-Test defeat at Adelaide and his participation in the Ashes series – plus his Ashes century – gave him much satisfaction in the autumn of his career.

Yet Makepeace still had one great achievement to come in first-class cricket: in the summer of 1926, at the age of 45, he scored 2,340 runs at an average of 48.75 as Lancashire won their first County Championship title for 22 years.

1921

'THE BIG SHIP' TUNES UP IN THE ENGINE ROOM

The Australian touring side of 1921 travelled to England on the steamship *Osterley*, which left Adelaide on 18 March. On board, too, were the England players vanquished 5–0 in the 1920–21 Ashes series. It must have made for a happy voyage for those Englishmen who knew that, in just over a couple of months, they would have to begin another series campaign against Warwick Armstrong and his fearsome team.

The colossus himself was due to turn 42 in the week before the first 1921 Test at Trent Bridge in late May. Armstrong knew that the coming tour was to be his swansong, and that he needed to be in the best physical condition possible to take on the labours of a four-month campaign so soon after the finish of the previous series.

At 22 stone, and knowing he could not afford to carry any surplus weight, he therefore left his fourteen men to relax and recuperate while he made daily trips to the ship's boilerhouse. There, no doubt to the delight of those whose working lives were spent in the bowels of the boat, the most instantly recognisable and most famous Australian cricket captain in history spent much of his travelling time shovelling coal.

And the proof that his radical training regime had worked came when he went on to send down 127 overs of his uncannily accurate slow-medium assortments in the five Tests, taking eight wickets, besides scoring useful runs that included innings of 77 and 28 not out in the Ashes-clinching, third-Test victory at Headingley. He was one of eight Australians to top 1,000 runs on that tour (both Macartney and Bardsley went past 2,000), and he took a total of 106 wickets.

In all, on his four tours of England in 1902, 1905, 1909 and 1921, 'The Big Ship' scored 5,974 runs in first-class matches at an average of 40.36, took 443 wickets at 16.45 and held 150 catches in his giant paws. He had a career run tally (from 1898 to 1921) of 16,158 at 46.83, including 45 centuries, and a wicket haul of 832 at 19.71.

Armstrong's final Test figures were also highly creditable: 2,863 runs at 38.68, with six hundreds, and 87 wickets at 33.59. It is as a captain and leader that he is best remembered, though, and perhaps his most appropriate memorial is the famous incident at the Oval, in the dying moments of a Test series which his all-conquering team had utterly dominated.

Leaving his team to organise itself, and indulge its lesser bowlers as the clock ticked down to a certain draw, Armstrong marked the end of his 50th Test and his career by withdrawing to the outfield, where he picked up a stray newspaper and began to read it – while play went on. When asked later about what he was reading, he replied (only partly in jest, to be sure): 'I wanted to see who we were playing!'

His actions, though, spoke even louder than his words. Despite being haughty and even bullying in manner and personality, the distinctly larger-than-life Armstrong was nevertheless a good-hearted man. Perhaps, in line with his own none-too-subtle character, this was the best way he could think of saying: 'My time is done, and my achievements will stand. We have pulverised England into complete submission. Now I can go into retirement and leave this Australian team to look after itself.'

THE STRANGE CASE OF CHARLIE PARKER

Charles Warrington Leonard Parker took more first-class wickets in cricket history than anybody bar Wilfred Rhodes and Kent's master tempter 'Tich' Freeman. But whereas Rhodes has passed into legend, and even Freeman's loopy leg-breaks earned him twelve England caps, the staunch countryman from Gloucestershire was given only a solitary chance at the highest level.

Charlie Parker's single Test was the rain-affected fourth match in the 1921 series, at Old Trafford, and as the all-conquering Australians were bowled out for 175 in their one innings of the game, slow left-armer Parker's figures were 28–16–32–2.

It is said that, in establishment circles, Parker's working-class country background militated against him. In one celebrated incident, at a Gloucestershire County Cricket Club function at a Bristol hotel in 1926, former England captain and MCC stalwart Sir Pelham Warner (then plain 'Plum') was accosted by Parker and accused of standing in the way of his career's rightful progress. He had to be pulled away from Warner by county team-mates. Whatever the rights and wrongs of what might have been said on that night, from this distance it does seem absurdly inexplicable that Parker was chosen just the once for England . . . and especially so at a time when Australia had established such a stranglehold over their oldest foe.

Perhaps it was his age, as he was already 38 at the time of his call-up – although he played in an era when Rhodes was still selected for international cricket at 52, Gunn at 50, Hobbs and Woolley at 47 and Strudwick and Hendren at 46. Perhaps it was simply that the under-pressure England selectors did not know which way to turn: they did, after all, call upon the ridiculous total of 30 different players for the five-match 1921 series. Or perhaps, as he himself suspected and at which he raged, Parker's face simply did not fit.

A craftsman and a perfectionist, and a terror in the Derek Underwood class on a rain-affected, 'sticky' pitch, Parker's career figures from 1903 to 1935 make jaw-dropping reading: 3,278 wickets at a cost of just 19.46 runs apiece. He took 200 or more wickets in a season on five occasions, with each of these feats coming after his sole Test cap, and sixteen times he topped 100. How on earth was this man only picked once for his country?

THE 1921 ONE-CAP CLUB

In defence of those who only picked Charlie Parker to play once for England, he was by no means the only one-cap wonder of that 1921 summer. The list of England's one-cap club of that particular Ashes series is, in chronological order: Tom Richmond (first Test), Alf Dipper, Jack Durston, John Evans (all second Test), Andy Ducat, Wally Hardinge (both third Test), Parker (fourth Test).

A sort of magnificent seven? Well, there was nothing magnificent about the selectorial thrashing about, but all seven men were fine sportsmen who achieved much in their lives and perhaps deserved better.

Richmond, of Nottinghamshire, was a roly-poly leg-spinner of slight build who, as the years progressed, grew rounder and rounder of girth. His first-class career stretched from 1912 until 1932, despite the fact that he was a negligible batsman and fielder, but between 1920 and 1926 he never took fewer than 113 wickets in a season. He had a good googly and spun the ball hard, and in his sole Test took 2 for 69 from 16 overs in Australia's first innings and 0 for 17 from three overs in their brief second innings as they ran out ten-wicket winners. Overall, his career brought him 1,176 first-class victims at 21.22 runs apiece.

Alf Dipper had a worthy 25-season career for his native Gloucestershire, mainly as an obdurate opening batsman of often underrated skill. In 1921 he was already 35 years old, and scored 11 and 40 in the Test at Lord's. In England's second innings he was joined in a second-wicket partnership of 94 by Frank Woolley, who played brilliant knocks of 95 and 93 in this match. But Dipper's typically gutsy effort was not enough either to keep him in the team, or to prevent England from slipping to an eight-wicket defeat.

Durston, meanwhile, was called up for the Lord's Test on the strength of his eleven wickets against the Australians for Middlesex a short time before, and like Dipper he did not perform at all badly. He took 4 for 102 in Australia's first innings of 342, and grabbed the wicket of the celebrated Charlie Macartney (for the second time in the game) as the tourists chased down a modest victory target in their second innings. Taking five of the twelve Aussie wickets to fall, however, at a cost of 136 from his total of 33.4 overs could not prevent Durston from being jettisoned either. His county Middlesex won the Championship in both 1920 and 1921, with the contributions of the six-foot-five-inch fast bowler Durston being one of the principal reasons for those successes, and he finished his first-class career at the age of 40 in 1933 with 1,329 wickets at 22.03. He was also a good enough goalkeeper to play for Brentford.

Evans, a former Oxford blue who had captained the University team in 1911, was 32 when he made his lone and, frankly, unexpected Test appearance. Like Durston, he was chosen mainly on the strength of a prior performance against the Australians; in his case, however, it was a mere 69 not out for MCC at Lord's and was not supported by the same weight of achievement in the domestic game. Evans, batting at six, scored just 4 and 14 in his sole Test and twice fell to the pace of Ted McDonald, who took eight wickets in the game. An attractive stroke-maker, Evans hit only six centuries in a sporadic first-class career spread over 21 years and in which he also represented Hampshire and Kent. In the First World War, he had escaped from a prisoner of war camp and later wrote a classic book about his adventures in *The Escaping Club*.

Ducat's call-up for the third Test at Headingley, which England lost by 219 runs to go a decisive 3–0 down, left the stalwart Surrey batsman thinking he was the victim of a practical joke. It took some time for him to be persuaded that none of his county colleagues were pulling his leg, but on figures alone he had more of a claim to Test recognition than his modesty allowed. By that time a soccer international, with six caps for England at half-back and an FA Cup winners' medal after leading Aston Villa to glory in 1920, Ducat was 35 and more than halfway through a first-class cricket career that, by its finish in 1931, was to bring him 23,373 runs – and 52 centuries – as a dapper stroke-maker at an average of 38.31.

Perhaps, though, his reaction to being called upon by England revealed an inner knowledge that he was not cut out for the highest stage: at Headingley, going in at four and then six, he scored just 3 and 2. He died at the crease at Lord's in 1942, at the age of 56, while batting in a wartime fixture between Home Guard units.

Like Ducat, Kent's Hardinge became a double international when he appeared in that Headingley defeat. He had played soccer once for England, as a centre-forward against Scotland in 1910, but he was also a fine batsman and more than useful slow left-arm spinner who had been central to Kent's Championship-winning teams of 1906, 1909, 1910 and 1913. He scored just 25 and 5 in his only Test, opening the batting in England's first innings with his great county team-mate Woolley, but in a first-class career stretching from 1902 to 1933 he amassed 33,519 runs at 36.51, with 75 centuries.

1924–25

THE CRUEL BLOW THAT COST
ENGLAND THE ASHES?

The 1924–25 series began on 19 December at the Sydney Cricket Ground. To find the day when England's chances of recapturing the Ashes ended, however, cricket historians insist that time is rewound to 3 July 1924 at the Oval. That was the day that Arthur Gilligan, England's new captain and the fastest bowler in the land, was hit over the heart while batting during the Gentlemen v Players match. Badly hurt by the delivery from Warwickshire fast bowler Harry Howell, who also played in five Tests for England in the early 1920s, Gilligan insisted on batting on; in fact, despite his severe discomfort, he made 112 in just over an hour and a half. So fearful was the blow, however, that medical opinion advised him to stop bowling fast – and the cheerful and charismatic Sussex skipper was never again the same force with the ball.

For the fate of English cricket, too, it was a tragic blow. Gilligan, who had turned 29 in December 1923, had taken 74 first-class wickets by the end of June 1924; after the incident he took just 29 more wickets in the season. Moreover, he had taken 26 wickets in his first five England appearances – including match figures of 11 for 90 in the opening Test of the 1924 series against South Africa. In fact, in his first bowling spell as captain of his country, Gilligan had finished with the astonishing figures of 6.3–4–7–6 as he and the debutant Maurice Tate (who took a wicket with his first ball in Tests) had skittled the South Africans for just 30 in 48 minutes and 75 balls of mayhem.

This was in reply to England's first innings of 438, in which Jack Hobbs and Herbert Sutcliffe had built the first of their fifteen three-figure opening stands – at the first attempt, as it was also Sutcliffe's debut Test – and although South Africa, following on, batted far more staunchly in their second innings to reach 390, they were beaten by an innings and eighteen runs.

Gilligan took a further 5 for 83, while the indefatigable Tate was into his 51st over when he finished off the South African resistance to finish with 4 for 103. Gilligan and Tate shared another nine wickets in the second Test as England moved towards an unbeatable 3–0 series lead – and England at last looked like having a cutting edge to their attack sharp enough to trouble the Australians.

Then, however, came Gilligan's accident. He bravely bowled in both the third and fifth Tests, but only took one more wicket in 44 overs. He was also forced to miss the fourth Test of that summer and, although he bowled in each of the five Tests on the 1924–25 tour, he took only ten wickets and broke down in his eighth over during the pivotal third Test (which England lost by just eleven runs) with a thigh muscle strain.

Tate, meanwhile, saw his own Herculean effort in Australia of 38 wickets at 23.18, from more than 316 eight-ball overs, buried beneath an ultimate 4–1 series defeat.

What if Gilligan had been able to bowl fast? What if Tate had been the supporting act with the new ball, and not expected to combine stock bowling with being the spearhead? So much else about the new-look, developing England side in 1924 and 1925 was good – especially, of course, the new-found opening alliance of Hobbs and Sutcliffe, the emergence of Tate as a major force, and the continued middle-order durability of Woolley and Hendren – but Gilligan's misfortune meant that England still did not possess enough power in their armoury to wrest back those Ashes.

THE LEGENDARY PARTNERSHIP THAT ALMOST NEVER WAS

Jack Hobbs very nearly did not tour Australia in 1924–25. In fact, he was thinking of giving up Test cricket altogether. It had been almost seventeen years since his first international match, and he was in his 43rd year. Thank goodness he was persuaded to stay!

At that stage of his career, for example, he had played 37 Test innings against Australia for an average of 53. How could he or anyone else know that he was about to begin a sequence of another 34 Ashes knocks . . . at an even higher average?

Perhaps it was his highly promising new partnership with Herbert Sutcliffe that clinched his decision to press on. The pair had played together in four Tests the previous summer, against South Africa, when their first three stands had been 136, 268 and 72. Now, their first seven partnerships against Australia were 157, 110, 283, 36, 90, 63 and 126. Sutcliffe became the first cricketer to hit four centuries in the same rubber, and only scores of 22 and 0 in the fifth and final Test brought his series average down to 81.55. Hobbs totalled 573 runs, to Sutcliffe's then record series aggregate of 734, and it was as hard on them as it was for the heroic Maurice Tate to finish on the losing side.

Hobbs, though, could see that the tide was at last turning – especially as England won their first Ashes Test since the Great War when they took the fourth Test at Melbourne by an innings and 29 runs (Hobbs 66, Sutcliffe 143). The third Test at Adelaide could easily have been England's, too, but for Tate suffering from blistered feet, Arthur Gilligan a bruised thigh and Tich Freeman a bruised wrist. Australia were thus able to stage a recovery from the depths of 119 for 6 on the opening day. In the end, England failed by just eleven runs to chase down a fourth-innings victory target of 375 and – what is more

– the first three Tests of the series were so hard fought that each needed a seventh day to reach completion.

Australia's all-round strength was such that Jack Ryder, who scored Ashes-clinching innings of 201 not out and 88 in the third Test at Adelaide, had not been able to get into the side for the opening two matches, nor had he made any of the 1921 Tests in England. Albert Hartkopf, meanwhile, a general practitioner who was a hard-hitting lower middle-order batsman and talented leg-break bowler, was brought into the second Test at Melbourne because the Australian selectors believed he would further strengthen their bowling. As it was, he took just one wicket for 134 in the match but, batting at number eight, he thumped 80 as the Aussies ran up a first-innings total of 600.

It was Hartkopf's only Test, but his runs were the vital difference: England, with Sutcliffe scoring 176 and 127 and Hobbs a first-innings 154, lost by a margin of 81 runs in another high-scoring affair.

1926

DAD'S ARMY ENGLAND WIN BACK THE ASHES

Because of bad luck with the weather, and the magnificent batting strength of both sides, the destiny of the Ashes in 1926 all came down to the fifth and final Test, at the Oval. It was designated as a timeless Test, so that a result could be guaranteed, but in the end it only took four days for England to emerge triumphant as holders of the Ashes once more.

In the end, England's margin of victory was a convincing 289 runs, but the game turned on one of the greatest exhibitions of batting ever seen: the second-innings opening partnership of 172, on a pitch made treacherous by an overnight thunderstorm, between Jack Hobbs and Herbert Sutcliffe.

England, trailing by 22 on first innings, had reached the close of the second day on 49 without loss. But, when noon on the Tuesday came and play was due to resume, the sun was shining and Hobbs and Sutcliffe were forced to deal with totally different – and devilishly difficult – conditions. The ball popped off the drying surface alarmingly, and Australia had the leg-spin and googlies of Clarrie Grimmett and Arthur Mailey, plus the off-breaks of Arthur Richardson to call upon.

No matter. Hobbs, reportedly taking his guard a foot outside of leg stump against Richardson's round-the-wicket attack, with four short-legs in place, showed such judgement of length and line and played the ball so late and softly that he managed to score runs as well as survive. By lunch, England were 161 without loss with the masterful Hobbs on 97 and the studious apprentice Sutcliffe on 53.

Hobbs was finally defeated by Jack Gregory's pace soon after the interval, but Sutcliffe kept going until being bowled by the last ball of the day for a magnificent 161. Maurice Tate's late thrash to 33 not out, from number nine, was the next best English score to the two peerless openers – but Australia, the game long taken away from them, still needed an impossible 415 to win.

Now came the moment that all England was waiting for – the return of the Ashes – and the urn was delivered by the youngest and oldest members of a team packed with experience. Wilfred Rhodes, recalled after a gap of more than five years at the age of 48, took 4 for 44 in support of a fearsomely fast burst from Harold Larwood, the 21-year-old tyro from Nottinghamshire making only his second Test appearance. Larwood's 3 for 34 gave him six wickets in the match – the same as Rhodes – and Tate (who took four wickets) at last had the pacey partner he deserved and desired.

England's triumph, however, had not been without some controversy. Arthur Carr, of Nottinghamshire, who had captained the team in the previous four Tests of the series but who had temporarily handed over the captaincy to Hobbs when taken ill with tonsillitis during the fourth Test at Old Trafford, was relieved of the job and dropped for the Oval decider. Percy Chapman, at 25 the third youngest member of the side, was appointed England captain and the three selectors ('Plum' Warner, Percy Perrin and Arthur Gilligan) decided to recall Larwood and George Geary as well as Chapman and Rhodes.

One of England's greatest victories vindicated their decision-making, of course, but it is especially interesting from a modern perspective to look at the ages of the players. Hobbs was 43, Sutcliffe 31, Frank Woolley 39, Patsy Hendren 37, Chapman 25, Greville Stevens 25, Rhodes 48, Geary 33, Tate 31, Larwood 21, and Herbert Strudwick 46. The average age of this famous side was pushing no less than 35.

1928–29

THE DON'S DEBUT TO FORGET

The most prolific batsman the world has ever seen endured the sort of international debut that nightmares are made of. Don Bradman, the man who was to finish his incredible career with batting averages of 95.14 (first class) and 99.94 (Tests), made a mere 18 in his first Test innings at Brisbane before being out lbw to Maurice Tate, and in his second had scored just a single run when caught by Percy Chapman at silly point off the slow left-arm of Jack 'Farmer' White. What is more, at the conclusion of the match on 5 December 1928, Australia had lost by the monumental margin of 675 runs.

England scored 521 and 342 for 8 declared, which represented an awful lot of leather-chasing for the 20-year-old prodigy from Bowral, while Australia were first blasted out for 122 by the pace and hostility of Harold Larwood, who took 6 for 32 to add to his merry first-innings 70 from number nine, and then humiliated as they crumbled to 66 all out.

By then, moreover, neither Jack Gregory nor Charles Kelleway was playing any part in the match – Gregory after suffering a career-ending knee cartilage injury during England's mammoth first innings, and Kelleway through illness that was to bring an end to his own illustrious Test career. Only Clarrie Grimmett, with match figures of 9 for 298 from a total of 84.1 overs, posed any kind of threat to the English batsmen on a perfect batting strip, and the reason why England were soon to be 4–0 up after four matches was immediately plain to see.

The Ashes' Strangest Moments

In Larwood and Maurice Tate they had the perfect, complementary spearhead of genuine pace and stout-hearted craft, and in the patience and skill and unflagging accuracy of the medium-paced George Geary and White, the slow left-armer from Somerset, they had the ideal supporting acts. White bowled more than 400 overs in the five-match series, taking 25 wickets, and the lion-hearted Tate 371.

Bradman, meanwhile, suffered the further pain and disappointment of being dropped (for the only time in his Test career) after the slaughter of Brisbane.

England won again in the second Test at Sydney, where Wally Hammond plundered 251 off the toothless Australian attack on his way to a record 905 runs in the series. Bradman, recalled for the third Test at the MCG and still down the order at six, made 79 and 112 but could not prevent a further, Ashes-deciding defeat for his team. In the next match, too, his 40 and 58 (run out) were not enough to squeeze Australia home in an exciting, tightly fought contest which England eventually won by twelve runs. Bradman's sizeable consolation, however, as this first chastening series came to a close, was the 123 and 37 not out he scored back at Melbourne to help Australia to a five-wicket win in a tortuous final Test that stretched into a record eighth day.

Jack Hobbs scored the last of his fifteen Test hundreds in this game, at the age of 46, and Hammond set his seemingly unsurpassable series run record aggregate. In little over a year, though, it was to be shattered by the phenomenon called Bradman. The tide, even in England's moment of glorious triumph, was already turning.

1930

COPLEY'S CATCH

It was the equivalent of an extra in a big Hollywood production suddenly getting the chance to speak the film's crucial line . . . and pulling it off in style. Sydney Copley's brilliant diving catch at Trent Bridge on 17 June 1930, to dismiss Stan McCabe for 49, was the moment that clinched victory for England in the opening Test of that summer's Ashes series.

Copley, a 24-year-old substitute fielder, played his only first-class match for Nottinghamshire a week later and was thus never in the spotlight again. Sadly for England, too, their substitute's moment of fame could not inspire them to retain the Ashes – because two men, Don Bradman and Clarrie Grimmett, who took 29 wickets overall, proved too potent.

But let's not forget Copley. A member of the Notts groundstaff, he was only on the field at all because Harold Larwood was suffering from a stomach upset and could bowl just five second-innings overs. Larwood had removed Aussie captain Bill Woodfull with the new ball before retiring to the pavilion, but Bradman had been joined by McCabe in a fourth-wicket stand worth 77 that had taken Australia on to 229 for 3. Their victory target was a distant 429, but this was Bradman and McCabe batting . . . and the England attack, without Larwood, was tiring and looking increasingly flimsy. But then McCabe tried to hit Maurice Tate and, from his position at mid-on, Copley 'made a lot of ground, took the ball at full-length and, although rolling over, retained possession' (*Wisden*).

Although Bradman went on to 131, England were then able to chip away through the probing seam-up of Tate and the spin of Dick Tyldesley and Walter Robins, and the Australians eventually ended up 93 runs adrift at 335 all out. Yet if the unknown Copley was the toast of England that night, the series was soon to be levelled at 1–1 and it was sorrows that needed to be drowned.

At Lord's, England totalled 425 and 375 and lost, with Duleepsinhji making 173 in the first innings and their captain Percy Chapman a defiant and robust 121 second time around. The main reason was Bradman, who scored 254 at a relentless pace to dominate successive stands of 231 with Woodfull (155) and 192 with Alan Kippax. That resulted in an Australian total of 729 for 6 declared – in the absence of Larwood, this time through injury, it must be remembered – which had been constructed so rapidly that there was still six hours of playing time left when Woodfull declared with his 304-run lead.

Ah yes, time. One of the changes brought in for the 1930 series was an extra day: before this year, all Tests in England (except deciding ones, which were deemed timeless) had been played over three days' duration. Now, this considerable amount of extra time proved to be tailor-made for Bradman in particular.

At Leeds in the next Test he made 334 (an innings which led the watching Wilfred Rhodes to call the 22-year-old 'the greatest batsman the world has ever seen') and, after a rare failure in the rain-wrecked fourth Test at Manchester, Bradman all but settled the final (still timeless) match at the Oval with another remarkable innings of 232. Bradman's series aggregate was a world record 974 runs at an average of 139.14, and the Oval witnessed an almost symbolic passing of the baton of batting mastery. This was Jack Hobbs' 61st and final Test. It was perhaps appropriate, too, that Herbert Sutcliffe made 161 and 54 to mark the last time he opened England's innings with his legendary partner, who was by then nearer to his 48th birthday than to his 47th of the previous December. Yet England were still bowled out for 405 and 251 to lose the match by an innings and 39 runs, and the Ashes with it.

Cruelly, given the timeless nature of the contest, even a rained-off fifth day could not save them.

It was the first time in 50 years of Test cricket at the Oval that an entire day's play had been lost to the weather; but, with the game resuming and being completed on the sixth, it mattered not. Added time, allied to Bradman's insatiability, had cost England dear.

1932–33

CRICKET'S MAN IN THE IRON MASK

Douglas Jardine. The austere, implacably determined English commander of the Bodyline series is still, more than 70 years on from cricket's biggest on-field controversy, a name to stir the passions on both sides of the cricketing world.

Scores of books, down the years, have weighed up the rights and wrongs of the 'leg-theory' tactics with which Jardine – chiefly through the immense stamina, pace, skill and accuracy of Harold Larwood, supported by his Nottinghamshire friend and team-mate Bill Voce and the courage of his close-in legside catchers – nullified the massive run-making threat of Donald Bradman, and seized back the Ashes. Hundreds of thousands of words have been written about the series which threatened to rupture the close blood ties between Britain and Australia. Many tens of thousands more have been penned to record the details of the on-field confrontations, and the reasons behind the actions and reactions of all the major characters in the drama.

On the Australian side, the magnificence of Stan McCabe's ultimately unavailing 187 not out in the opening Test at Sydney, the courageous and publicly uncomplaining resilience of captain Bill Woodfull in the line of fire, and the emergence of Bill O'Reilly as a bowler of rare ability, stand out as beacons of high achievement in a truly testing environment.

In a series which, in a cricket sense, contained much that was brilliant as well as brutal, there was also from the English side the cool batting class of Herbert Sutcliffe and Wally

Hammond, the legendary rise from a Brisbane hospital bed of fourth-Test batting hero Eddie Paynter, the speed of Gubby Allen (who refused throughout to bowl Bodyline) and the skilful slow left-arm variations of Hedley Verity. Overshadowing all, though, remains the most potent weapon on view and the man who wielded it: Larwood, and Jardine.

Even with the Ashes won, following the remarkable victory in Brisbane which put England 3–1 ahead, Jardine was so obsessed with using the very presence of Larwood to intimidate Bradman that, in the second innings of the final Test back at Sydney, he would not permit his strike bowler to leave the field with a broken bone in his foot while Bradman remained at the crease. Keeping up the pretence that Larwood was suffering merely from cramp after a typically fierce new-ball spell in which he had accounted for Vic Richardson and struck Bradman a heavy blow on the upper arm, Jardine waited until Bradman had been bowled by Verity for an aggressive 71 before allowing Larwood to hobble off alongside the departing chief target of his uncompromising tactics.

Bradman's approach for most of this series had been to seek every chance to score – often jumping around the crease to aim unorthodox strokes and even playing 'tennis' shots to the short-pitched bowling on occasions – in a seemingly twin desire to hit runs quickly and avoid getting hit. Because of this rather cavalier attitude, and despite his series average of 56, many observers reckon Bradman played right into Jardine's hands.

Jardine himself, however, very nearly did not figure in either the third and fourth Tests of this tumultous series . . . because of his own desire not to allow anything to stand in the way of the team's success.

In the lead-up to both Tests, which England won to secure the regaining of the Ashes, Jardine proposed that he himself should stand down from the team. The reason was his lack of form with the bat, allied to the fact that the Nawab of Pataudi, despite scoring 102 in the opening Test, was being omitted from the side to allow for Paynter's elevation. Jardine had scored just 1 and 0 in the lost second Test, at Melbourne, in addition to his stodgy 27 at Sydney. Before the third Test at

Adelaide, which was to provide the very epicentre of the seismic Bodyline controversy, Jardine left the room during the selection meeting after asking for his own position to be discussed. The tour selection panel unanimously voted for him to retain his place and, moreover, to move up to open the innings.

Despite an iron-willed second-innings 56 at Adelaide, however, Jardine once more ordered that his place in the team should be debated for the crunch fourth Test. Again, though, the three senior players on the selection committee alongside Jardine and tour manager 'Plum' Warner – Sutcliffe, Hammond and Bob Wyatt – would not hear of the skipper dropping himself. Although Hammond was always an opponent of fast leg-theory for purely moral and aesthetic reasons, his attitude of unswerving loyalty to the England cause in 1932–33 was typical of a squad also containing other 'conscientious objectors' such as Allen and Pataudi.

Whatever else he was, Jardine inspired the total respect of his playing peers and their devotion to the job in hand. Perhaps, through all the controversy and cordite of the 1932–33 tour, it was only his closest colleagues in the England dressing room who saw the real character behind the caricature of his unbending, arrogant, autocratic public face.

Perhaps, too, there was just one public moment when the Jardine mask slipped and the passion of a man utterly determined to destroy the Bradman legend and take back the Ashes was revealed: when Bill Bowes bowled the Don first ball for 0 in Bradman's first innings of the series, in the second Test, to an ugly under-edged attempted pull, Jardine lost his self-control for a few joyous seconds in an ecstatic reaction to this piece of outrageous good fortune. In the words of Bowes himself, the seemingly cold and emotionless England captain 'clasped both his hands above his head and was jigging around like an Indian doing a war dance'.

FRIENDSHIPS FORGED IN THE HEAT OF BATTLE

Amid all the bad blood of the 1932–33 Ashes conflagration, one moment above all stands out as the iconic image of the Bodyline battle. It is the staggering figure of Bert Oldfield, with his bat flung down and his gloved hands raised up to his face, caught on both still and film cameras reeling away from the crease after being struck a sickening blow by yet another short ball from Larwood.

Oldfield, the Australian wicket-keeper, had made a gutsy 41 in the third Test at Adelaide when he top-edged a hurried attempted pull into his temple. Larwood was not bowling Bodyline at this time, and nor had he been when Bill Woodfull had been struck a terrible blow over the heart on the previous day, but the Australian crowd was as near to a riot as it ever came. What the furious spectators could not hope to hear, however, amid the din and in the chilling yet white-hot moments that followed, was Larwood rushing up to Oldfield to enquire if he was all right – and Oldfield replying, through his pain and shock: 'It wasn't your fault, Harold.'

The batsman had 'lost' the ball against the Adelaide Oval's low sightscreen for a fatal millisecond. As Oldfield retired hurt, to play no further part in the game, and Australia's fading hopes went with him, no one on the ground that day would have believed it possible that he would live to count Harold Larwood as one of his firmest friends. It is one of sport's greatest ironies that the man who nearly killed Oldfield on the field of play – his fracture of the skull was just an inch away from a spot on the right temple which would have meant almost certain death – was to become a pallbearer at his actual funeral more than 43 years later in 1976.

Larwood's decision to emigrate to Australia with his young family in 1950 came after words of encouragement to do so from another of his Bodyline adversaries, opening batsman Jack Fingleton. And the reason the former scourge of the Aussies settled so quickly and so contentedly in Sydney was the friendship he found from the likes of Fingleton, Oldfield, Stan McCabe and Bill O'Reilly.

Oldfield, by the way, already had a steel reinforcement plate lodged in another part of his skull as a result of being severely wounded during the First World War. Serving in the 15th Field Ambulance, he was the only survivor of a five-man stretcher party hit by a German shell. Buried in mud for hours, due to the force of the explosion, he suffered head and back injuries which, allied to shell-shock, meant he had then needed to spend several months recuperating in hospitals in France and England.

THE SICK MAN WHO BECAME AN OVERNIGHT ASHES HERO

Eddie Paynter did not play in the first two Ashes Tests of the 1932–33 series, but by the time England clinched the 'return' of the urn by winning the fourth match of the rubber at Brisbane, he had become a national hero.

The reason has passed into cricketing legend. Paynter, called up for the third Test in Adelaide, had already made a vital 77 there and had shaken off an ankle injury to keep his place for Brisbane. But, as Australia began the crucial Test by amassing a first innings of 340 in baking heat, Paynter felt less and less well. By the second day of the game he had a temperature of 102 and was taken to Brisbane General Hospital where acute tonsillitis was diagnosed.

On the next day, the match's Sunday rest day, Paynter remained in bed in hospital and later described how the hours passed in a 'sickly maze' of pill-popping, passages of sleep, and visits from team-mates who included Douglas Jardine, the captain. The skipper had, characteristically, urged the little

Lancashire left-hander to make himself available to bat whatever his condition, but doctors at the hospital still felt – on examining him again the following morning – that he was too ill to play any further part in the match.

England began the third day looking comfortable on 99 without loss in reply to the sizeable but hardly intimidating Australian first-innings score, but soon wickets began to fall with alarming regularity as spinners O'Reilly and Ironmonger put a stranglehold on the England batsmen, still in withering heat. Fast bowler Bill Voce, sidelined for this match because of injury, was with Paynter in his hospital ward when the pair heard on the radio commentary from the ground that two more wickets had fallen. Paynter decided to act, and instructed Voce to order a taxi.

Wrapping himself in his dressing gown, he ignored the cries of the ward sister to get back into bed and, with Voce, was driven to the Gabba ground. They arrived just after the tea interval, to the astonishment of Jardine and the rest of the England players. But, soon after Paynter had changed into his cricket gear and strapped on his pads, he found himself walking out to the middle on the fall of Gubby Allen's wicket. England were 216 for 6 and Les Ames, the not-out batsman, greeted Paynter's appearance with bemusement bordering on disbelief.

The new ball was now due, too, and Ames was dismissed with the total having moved on to just 225, but somehow Paynter hung on. Joined by Larwood, he concentrated merely on survival, being too devoid of strength to attempt to hit the ball very hard, and by the close had batted 75 minutes for his unbeaten 24. Larwood was out shortly before the end of play for the day, for 23, but Hedley Verity had also held on stubbornly and England were still in the game at 271 for 8.

Paynter, putting his pyjamas back on in the dressing room, was then driven back to hospital 'in a bit of a daze' – where he spent a third night. The following morning, after a good sleep, he felt appreciably better and found – when he resumed his innings – that attacking strokes were now back on the agenda. With Verity, a sound number ten, resisting strongly and enjoying some moments of good fortune, Paynter's decision to take the game back to Australia made for thrilling cricket.

Twice play was stopped for the Lancastrian to take more medicine, but by now it was the Australian bowlers who were beginning to feel a little bit sick. Paynter's jaunty stroke-play took him on to a remarkable 83 before he finally lifted a catch, and his 92-run ninth-wicket stand with Verity, who remained 23 not out when the innings almost immediately ended with the fall of last man Tommy Mitchell to O'Reilly, had even earned England the unlikeliest of first-innings leads (of sixteen runs). Despite his by now weary condition, Paynter even had enough adrenalin pumping through his ravaged system to insist on fielding for a couple of hours as Australia began a second innings that was to end with their dismissal for just 175.

Fittingly, on the sixth day, and after a fourth night spent in the by now familiar surroundings of Brisbane General, it was Paynter who entered with England just 22 runs from victory on 138 for 4 in their second innings, and he proceeded to pull O'Reilly for four and then swing a full toss from McCabe for the six which clinched both the match and the Ashes. The previous night, too, he had been woken at midnight to receive a telephone call from his wife May, who had been persuaded to perform what was then regarded as the miraculous action of speaking to her hero husband from her Manchester home through the auspices of the publicity-seeking organisers of the Telephones and Telegraphs Exhibition.

Amid the rancour of Bodyline, this story of the sick man who had risen in triumph from his hospital bed had caught the imagination: even Australian cricket-lovers initiated a special testimonial collection for the small 30-year-old Lancastrian who had dashed all their team's remaining Ashes hope.

1934

THE FLAMES OF BODYLINE ARE EXTINGUISHED . . . BY ENGLAND

It seems truly remarkable, looking back, that Harold Larwood never played for England again following his Ashes-winning heroics in 1932–33 . . . and that, for the 1934 visit of the Australians to England, he and Bill Voce were excluded from the series by the actions of the English cricket authorities.

How different it might have been if Douglas Jardine had still been England captain, with a record of nine wins and just one defeat from his fifteen Tests in charge, but he had voluntarily given up the job at the end of March 1934, immediately after leading England to a 2–0 series victory in India, in order to marry and begin a new career as a cricket journalist. His first assignment was to report on the 1934 Ashes series.

Larwood, meanwhile, had bowled hardly a ball during the 1933 summer as he took time to recover from the broken bone in his foot that he had suffered at Sydney while helping England to clinch the 1932–33 Ashes series by a crushing 4–1 margin. He had also undergone surgery on the troublesome foot during the winter of 1933–34, but by May 1934 he was playing again for Nottinghamshire. He was not yet 30 and, if not now operating at quite the blistering pace of the Bodyline series, he was still England's most feared and most experienced strike bowler.

Voce, too, was taking clusters of wickets in county cricket . . . so, surely, even without Jardine to lead them, the matchless Notts pair would be the first names down on the England selectors' notepads?

Sadly, however, things were not quite so simple. Not by a long chalk. English cricket in the early summer of 1934 was dominated, for those that ran it, by the issue of ensuring that the 1934 Ashes series passed off without any problems. Politics had taken over. The Ashes, of course, needed defending. But, unlike in 1932–33, the MCC was determined not to do so at any cost. The memory of Bodyline simply had to be buried. England, in short, promised Australia that there would be no leg-theory in the 1934 series – which meant, in turn, that Larwood and Voce could only play if certain assurances were given by them.

Approached some time before the first Ashes Test began on 8 June, Larwood was initially told by the MCC that he would not be selected for England until he issued a formal apology to them for the nature of his bowling in the 1932–33 series. Incredulous, Larwood replied: 'Apologise? What for?' Had he not received congratulatory telegrams from the MCC itself after the first, fourth and fifth Tests of the previous Ashes campaign? Unsurprisingly, he refused.

Larwood's absence from the opening Test of 1934, which was won by Australia, was officially put down to his continuing foot injury problems, but his 5 for 66 for Nottinghamshire against Sussex soon exposed that lie. Then, five days before the start of the second Test, at Lord's, a furious Larwood authorised an exclusive first-person column in the *Sunday Dispatch*, in which he wrote: 'It is time the public knew the truth . . . I have made up my mind not to play against the Australians in this or any of the Tests. I am unrepentant about leg theory. There is a big hush-hush campaign to bury leg theory and brand me as a dangerous and unfair bowler . . .' Voce, meanwhile, also vented his spleen in another Sunday newspaper column.

The Notts captain, the outspoken Arthur Carr, rounded on the English authorities and said: 'The rulers of the game have so completely deserted him.' And so the 1934 series ground on. Verity's fifteen wickets squared the series at Lord's but the Australians were unfortunate not to go 2–1 up when rain saved England after Bradman had smashed 304 in the fourth Test at Headingley and added 388 with Bill Ponsford.

Even now, at 1–1, and with just the Oval to follow, there was a groundswell of popular opinion for Larwood and Voce to come riding to England's aid in the hour of need. But it just wasn't going to happen – especially after a huge row broke out during the Australians' visit to play Nottinghamshire at Trent Bridge in the week leading up to the fifth and final Test.

Larwood, by now thoroughly disillusioned, asked to be left out of his county's team. Voce, by contrast, stated his intention both to play . . . and to let the Aussies have both barrels. The result was, uniquely in that summer, a Bodyline field to a true Bodyline bowler – and Voce ended up with 8 for 66 in an Australian first-innings total of just 237. His victims included Woodfull, Kippax, McCabe, Bill Brown and Len Darling and, when he finished the second day by bowling two overs consisting of eleven short-pitched deliveries at the start of the tourists' second innings, the Aussies issued a formal complaint. Mysteriously, in an incident Voce himself was later to allege was deliberately manufactured by the rattled authorities, the big left-armer failed to appear on the field the following morning, citing an injury.

In the final Test, Bradman scored 244 and Ponsford 266. They put on 451 in a mere 316 minutes, and Australia's first innings reached 701. England lost by 562 runs, and the Ashes were Australia's again.

A BIRTHDAY DOUBLE FOR WOODFULL

Coincidence – happy, unhappy or strange – has always played its mischievous or malevolent part in the fascination of sport. Few coincidences of the happy variety can, however, match that which was experienced by Bill Woodfull, the captain of Australia, in his 35th and final Test, at the Oval on 22 August 1934.

That it was on his 37th birthday that his Australian team won the deciding match of the series by a huge margin of 562 runs, to clinch the regaining of the Ashes, was notable enough. But what made it remarkable was that it was the second time in four years that Woodfull had won the Ashes on his birthday.

In 1930, also at the Oval, Australia had completed an innings and 39-run victory on 22 August – Woodfull's 33rd birthday – to take that Ashes series by a 2–1 margin. It was his first series as Australian captain and now, four years on, here he was again celebrating his birthday with another 2–1 series win to regain the Ashes for his country. It was a unique double and Woodfull, having led Australia for the 25th time, was able to go contentedly into his cricketing retirement with 2,300 Test runs at 46.00 to his name, and 13,388 overall in first-class matches at the eye-catchingly high average of 64.99.

Seven of his 49 first-class hundreds came in Tests and Woodfull, through his high standards of behaviour both on and off the field, and by his dignified deportment throughout the Bodyline controversy of 1932–33 especially, had earned himself a reputation as one of cricket's best and most statesmanlike of leaders. What is more, he enjoyed his sporting retirement by moving full-time into education as a much-respected Melbourne schoolteacher, and it was for this work above all that he was awarded the OBE in 1963 – just two years before his death at the age of 67.

Interestingly, back in late 1934, Woodfull had declined the offer of a knighthood for his services to cricket. He felt his teaching career was the more important.

1936-37

THE DAY OF TWO FIRST-INNINGS DECLARATIONS

The greatest lesson to be learned from history is that it repeats itself. But surely England's suffering bowlers did not deserve the fate which again awaited them at the hands of Don Bradman's mighty bat during the 1936–37 Ashes tour.

In England in 1934 the Don had begun that series with (for him) a run of low scores: in fact, his first five innings of the rubber brought him just 133 runs, and he didn't reach 50 once. Unfortunately for England, however, as Australia also recovered from a shaky start to win the series, Bradman's last three innings were 304, 244 and 77.

Now, as England began their 1936–37 campaign by storming into a 2–0 lead after just two Tests, Bradman again struggled for early-series form. Once more, uncannily, his first five innings of the rubber brought him only 133 runs – although an 82 in the second innings of the second Test at Sydney went some way to making up for ducks both there and in the opening match in Brisbane. England might have protested that they still didn't know what was coming, but it wasn't as if they had not been warned; and, indeed, Bradman's remaining knocks as Australia turned around the series to finish 3–2 winners were the little matter of 270, 26, 212 and 169.

What is more, Bradman was by now in his first series as captain of Australia and had needed a huge amount of good fortune with the weather (as well as his own batting genius) to stand the third Test at Melbourne – and with it the series – on its head.

Soon after tea on the opening day, and after winning the toss, Australia were in a sorry state at 130 for 6 – with Bradman gone for 13 to a poor stroke. Then, however, came rain and (with pitches not being covered in those days) England were forced to operate at the end of the interrupted day with a wet and slippery ball. Australia rallied to 181 for 6 at the close but, by the start of the second day and after more rain, the drying Melbourne pitch had turned into a feared 'sticky dog'.

Three quick wickets confirmed to Bradman that his luck had changed; immediately, he declared Australia's first innings closed on 200 for 9 and decided that his bowlers needed to get to work as quickly as possible themselves on the gluepot of a pitch. England, soon 14 for 2, briefly rallied through Wally Hammond and Maurice Leyland – with Hammond demonstrating the previous mastery of a Jack Hobbs or a Herbert Sutcliffe to get to 32. But, from 56 for 2 and then 68 for 3, as both Hammond and Leyland fell to brilliant short-leg catches, England collapsed to 76 for 9 before – too late – their own captain, Gubby Allen, decided to seize the moment himself and declare.

It was the first time in Test history that both first innings of a match had been declared closed, but Allen should have acted sooner. As it was, Bradman sent in his three tailenders to bat at one, two and three in a second innings that had time to decline only to 3 for 1 by the close – and, after a dry rest day which did England even fewer favours, he himself waited until the pitch had almost completely dried out before marching in at number seven with his team having struggled to 97 for 5.

The result was a record sixth-wicket stand worth 346 with Jack Fingleton, who had also dropped down from opener to number six and supported Bradman's majestic double century with a highly valuable innings of 136. Bradman's 270, meanwhile, had not only turned the tide of the series – it had also converted his own previous trickle of runs into an all too familiar flood.

A POIGNANT POSTSCRIPT

Scorecards, to cricket lovers, are revealing and revered documents at the best of times: to be pored over in the newspapers every summer morning, and to be studied again with a sigh or a smile when years have passed and a trip down a nostalgic lane is being sought. Yet, in the whole history of the game – and certainly that of the Ashes – can there ever have been a more poignant line in a scorecard than the following from 1937, which was recorded as Australia ran up an Ashes-clinching first innings total of 604 in the fifth and final Test at the Melbourne Cricket Ground?

It reads: R G Gregory c Verity b Farnes 80, and it was a scorebook entry to preface the cold reality of an approaching world war and a ten-year interruption to the epic Ashes story.

Ross Gregory, who had turned 21 on the first day of the Test – 26 February – came in at number six, with Australia already in command at 346 for 4, and proceeded to add a further 161 with Jack Badcock, whose 118 followed up centuries by both Bradman and McCabe. But the big-hearted giant fast bowler Ken Farnes, of Essex, eventually numbered the talented young Gregory among the splendid six wickets he took for 96 amid the stroke-making carnival being played out on a featherbed of a pitch.

The terrible relevance that it should be Hedley Verity, equally well loved and admired, who took the catch only became apparent on 31 July 1943, when Captain Verity of the Green Howards died from wounds sustained when leading his company into battle during the Allied invasion of Sicily. He was 38.

For, just over a year earlier, in June 1942, Sergeant Observer Gregory of the Australian Air Force was just 26 when he died on active service in Assam. Pilot Officer Farnes, meanwhile, was 30 and serving his country in the RAF when he was killed in a flying accident over Oxfordshire on 20 October 1941.

1938

WAS HAMMOND THE REASON?

Reg Sinfield was a fine, solid and dependable county cricketer but was always lacking the extra quality required for international recognition. And yet, at the age of 37, Sinfield was chosen to play in the opening Test match of the 1938 Ashes series, at Trent Bridge.

Batting at number nine, a man good enough to have been a long-time opening batsman for Gloucestershire came in with England on 597 for 7 and was soon lbw to Bill O'Reilly for 6. On a featherbed of a pitch, which allowed Australia twice to pass 400 despite having to follow on, Sinfield then spent the rest of his only Test bowling his canny little off-spinners and off-cutters to an Australian batting line-up in which Stan McCabe made a first-innings 232 and both Bill Brown and Don Bradman scored second-innings centuries.

Sinfield took 1 for 51 from 28 first-innings overs and then 1 for 72 from 35 more second time around, and yet he was still rewarded with his little moment in the sun. Bradman, on 51, edged him to Les Ames behind the stumps and an honest journeyman of the game could celebrate taking the scalp of the world's most feared batsman.

But is it more than a coincidence that Sinfield's selection came in Walter Hammond's first match as England captain? Hammond, having given up his professional status the previous winter to become the first of his kind to turn amateur, had thus 'qualified' to assume the job of England captaincy that – by the sheer force of his immortal talent and god-like persona – was his for the taking.

Hammond, who has been rated by many commentators (including C B Fry and Sir Leonard Hutton) even above Bradman and Hobbs as the greatest batsman who ever lived, was a complex man – but his love of his adopted county Gloucestershire never wavered. Rootless, classless and with a shyness and lack of confidence in public that many took for aloofness and moodiness, Hammond always found it difficult to forge close relationships with those he played with.

Sinfield, however, was one of the salt-of-the-earth characters in the Gloucestershire team who allowed Hammond to feel at home, and relaxed. It was only later in his life that he learned of Hammond's true admiration for his positive and friendly attitude, and for the grit and honesty which he brought to his cricket.

So was this call-up, out of the blue, Wally's way of saying thanks? Pure conjecture, perhaps, but stranger things have happened, and Hammond was always someone with firm beliefs about the right way to play the game – and the value of cricket's accepted standards and principles. In pre-war English county cricket, no one was more universally admired in terms of his character than Reg Sinfield, who by 1938 was the ultimate old pro.

In the 1920s Hammond – the son of an Army officer killed in the First World War and brought up as a grammar-school boy – found it difficult to accept the social divide in which the professionals were addressed by their surnames by the 'ruling' amateurs, and changed in a separate dressing room. It was not without significance that Hammond was alone in calling his county captain at Gloucestershire, Bev Lyon, by his Christian name rather than by the accepted, formal 'sir'. It is a fact, too, that he was, by his very status in the game and by his bearing, thought of more as an amateur than a professional: otherwise, he would never have been allowed the unique opportunity suddenly to become an amateur after more than fifteen years in the professional ranks. Hammond, who ironically had many times found himself being referred to as 'Mr Hammond' by young fellow professionals, was the prime mover in breaking down the social barriers of the age so that, in Len Hutton in 1952, England could soon have a professional cricketer as her captain.

Back in 1938, though, in his first experience of being granted the power of national leadership, did the notoriously uncommunicative Hammond express his feelings in the best way he could by symbolically picking Reg Sinfield to take on the Aussies just that one time? It would be nice to think so.

HOW THE STAGE WAS SET FOR A LEGEND TO BE BORN

One of the most famous of all cricket innings, and one of the most famous scorecards, belong to the Oval Ashes Test of 1938. But the story that lies behind Len Hutton's 364 and England's mammoth 903 for seven declared is not so widely appreciated.

Australia went into the match already assured of retaining the Ashes after going an unbeatable 1–0 up in the series with a five-wicket win in the previous Test at Headingley. That victory owed much to Bill O'Reilly's ten-wicket match haul and a brilliant first-innings 103 by Don Bradman. But England captain Wally Hammond was determined to level the series against a team led by his great rival. Both skippers gambled on winning the toss and batting their opponents out of a game that was scheduled to be a timeless Test and, therefore, was bound to be played out to a finish.

England picked just three front-line bowlers, and Australia had only two of proper Test class in O'Reilly and his fellow spinner Fleetwood-Smith. Hammond won the gamble and instructed his batsmen to concentrate on crease occupation. Hutton, young and keen, set out to do just that and, with Maurice Leyland, put on 382 for the second wicket. Hammond then came in to stroke 59 as another 135 was added. Even a middle-order collapse which claimed Eddie Paynter for 0 and Denis Compton for 1 could not halt England's relentless progress towards Test cricket's highest total. Hutton, meanwhile was on his way to eclipsing Hammond's own Test record individual score of 336 not out.

Hutton was joined in a further partnership of 125 by Joe Hardstaff junior, departing finally at 770 when he was sixth out. Even then, though, Hardstaff was determined to surge on, having been urged by his captain to 'play steady' when he had gone in at 555 for 5. He eventually finished on 169 not out, while Hammond only put a stop to the slaughter and prevented a final assault on the 1,000 due to injuries suffered in the field by Jack Fingleton and Bradman himself. Opening batsman Fingleton pulled a muscle, and Bradman chipped a bone in his foot when he turned his ankle bowling. Neither was fit to bat, and that is the only reason Hammond declared at 903.

England eventually ran out winners by an innings and 579 runs, bowling out a depleted and distinctly fed-up Australia for 201 and 123. And, in the end, the match only lasted four days.

1946–47

THE LONG AND SILENT DRIVE WHICH SAID SO MUCH

Cricket's fates turned cruelly on one of the game's greatest when Walter Hammond agreed to lead England's 1946–47 Ashes tour in the strongly held belief that it was a service to the post-war game that he simply had to perform.

Hammond saw the tour in an almost crusading light, and his acceptance of the invitation to continue as England's captain sprang from his desire to provide clear leadership in the tough rebuilding years that the game faced in the late 1940s. Many of England's long-established players had retired in the six lost years of the Second World War; some, like Hedley Verity, Ken Farnes and Maurice Turnbull, had fallen. Those new, younger cricketers who were emerging lacked the breadth of experience of match-play that 'normal' generations take for granted.

Hammond, at his absolute peak when war intervened, had played a vital part in maintaining morale by starring in many wartime matches, both at home and abroad, while fulfilling his duties as an RAF training officer. Now, at 43 and having played first-class cricket since 1920, he saw it as his duty to undertake one last Ashes battle. The opening Test of the 1946–47 series, however, undermined all his good intentions and ambitions and – on a 900-mile drive south to Sydney afterwards – left him literally staring into space.

Hammond, usually a charming companion if somewhat of a loner, had begun the tour full of form on the field and in fine spirits off it. He had then suffered the twin pain of seeing details of his forthcoming divorce splattered across all the Australian newspapers and the news that the woman who was to become his beloved second wife was unhappy at home. With more than six months of the tour still to go, Hammond was already having to steel himself to deal with these unsettling developments in his personal life even as the first Test got under way at Brisbane. He was also increasingly troubled by fibrositis, and was ultimately forced to miss the fifth and final Test and sit out the last five weeks of the tour because of his worsening condition. But what happened in the very first session of that opening Test match was to prove even more difficult to take.

Hammond himself had snapped up Arthur Morris at slip, off Alec Bedser, to give England a vital early breakthrough and leave Australia at 9 for 1. Don Bradman, coming in as usual at number three, was decidedly ill at ease, and was close to being dismissed on a number of occasions. When he had made just 28, moreover, England believed he had sliced a full-length ball from Bill Voce that then flew almost shoulder-high to Jack Ikin, standing alongside Hammond at second slip. Bradman, however, stood his ground as Ikin celebrated, clearly believing he had hit the ball into the ground, and England were forced to make an appeal to the umpire. It was turned down.

Hammond himself reacted to the incident with characteristic dignity, saying to Bradman afterwards: 'I thought it was a catch, but I may have been wrong.' England, though, were livid – and their mood became decidedly blacker as Bradman, thus reprieved, went on to score 187 and add 276 for the third wicket with Lindsay Hassett.

Yet, even after Australia's first-innings total had reached 645, things were about to get much worse for England. Following torrential thunderstorms on successive nights, only 99 minutes' play was possible on the third day, and three more hours were lost on the fourth. The second storm had left the whole ground flooded, with winds of more than 80 miles per hour also whipping away the covers while giant hailstones bombarded the stands and outfield.

Unfortunately for Hammond, however, the storms did not last long enough for the match to be abandoned. Moreover, England were twice condemned to bat on a sticky pitch, and in conditions that had utterly changed they were bowled out first for 141 and then for 172 to lose by an innings and 332 runs. In the end, England lost their last fifteen wickets in three and a half hours . . . and Australia clinched victory at 4.40 p.m. on the final afternoon.

Hammond, with 32 and 23, made more runs than any other England batsman and reportedly batted with incredible skill in the near-impossible conditions. But, as he drove away from the ground soon after 5 p.m., he knew that the wretched luck his team had endured in Brisbane meant that the task of bringing home the Ashes was suddenly a far stiffer one. He also knew that Bradman's 'life' had relieved the pressure on the 38-year-old Australian captain on his own international comeback. Indeed, Bradman himself later conceded that his decision to carry on playing Test cricket until 1948 was based on that century in Brisbane.

All this, plus thoughts of home and the latest chapter of what had sometimes been his agonising search for personal happiness, was clearly on Hammond's mind as he drove through the night from Brisbane to Sydney. His passengers on that long car ride were Len Hutton and Cyril Washbrook, the England openers, and they both often recalled it as one of the strangest experiences of their lives. Hammond drove fast, too, in what his travelling companions reported as almost a trance-like state, although neither felt anything other than safe with him at the wheel. The vast distance was covered with barely a stop, with Hammond seemingly oblivious to fatigue. And their captain spoke to them hardly at all for the 900 miles; his only words were repeated requests to light up a cigarette for him, and commands for them to locate petrol station attendants on the several occasions when a low fuel tank necessitated a short break in the journey.

Perhaps, to understand and explain Hammond's anguished state of mind as he drove relentlessly through the early December Australian night, one has to fast-forward four months: on 9 April, after Australia had kept the Ashes by a 3–0 margin, he arrived back in England, and in London on 10 April he married his second wife, Sybil Ness-Harvey.

1948

WHEN LAKER WAS POWERLESS TO STOP A RUN FLOOD

Australia's supreme mastery during the 1948 Ashes series, which they ended up winning 4–0, is best illustrated by events at the fourth Test at Headingley. England, already 2–0 down, were so determined to try to get back into the series that they actually declared their second innings when in a position close to impregnable strength, setting Australia 404 to win in 344 minutes . . . and then saw their opponents run up 404 for three from 114.1 overs, on a pitch taking spin, to win the match by seven wickets. Just how remarkable was this achievement is indicated by the fact not only that Australia's score stood as the highest fourth-innings total made to win a Test until 1975–76, when India made 406 for 4 to beat West Indies in Trinidad, but that only once in Test history had a side even made 300 runs to win a match before.

In truth, the Australians won at a canter with fifteen minutes to spare, Don Bradman putting on 301 in just 217 minutes with Arthur Morris. It was the Don's 29th and final Test hundred, and his nineteenth against England, and his unbeaten 173 – containing 29 boundaries – provided the crowning glory of his astonishing career. Morris scored 182, and their great match-winning partnership underlined the fact that Bradman's 1948 'Invincibles' seemed to be able to win matches from any position.

Beneath the black and white reality of the scorebook, however, is the grim fact that England's selectors themselves contributed to the Australian victory . . . by not picking a recognised spinner, and preferably a leg-spinner, to bowl alongside Jim Laker.

Off-spinner Laker was, in 1948, nowhere near the force he was to become in the 1950s, but here he was being asked to spin out Bradman's Australians in favourable conditions but with only the part-time leg-spin of Denis Compton and Len Hutton in support. Early on, indeed, Morris should have been stumped off Compton and Bradman was missed at slip after misreading a Compton googly. He was also dropped at both 50 and 108. Compton's solitary success, the early caught and bowled dismissal of Lindsay Hassett, eventually came at a cost of 82 runs from his fifteen overs. Hutton's four exploratory overs were thrashed for 30 runs. Laker, meanwhile, did manage eleven maidens but also leaked 93 runs in total from his 32 wicketless overs. Australia's runs had come at a rate of 74 an hour.

THE MOST FAMOUS DUCK IN HISTORY

It is the richest of ironies that one of the most remembered moments in the career of cricket's most relentless run-gatherer is Don Bradman's second-ball duck in his very last Test innings. What is not so widely recalled, though, is the gleeful reaction of two of Bradman's former Test-playing colleagues in the Oval press box.

Having already received a prolonged standing ovation, Bradman reached the wicket to three cheers from the England players orchestrated by their captain, Norman Yardley. Eventually the Don settled down to face the bowling of Eric Hollies. The England spinner's first ball was a leg-break, to which Bradman played defensively forwards with a dead bat. The second was a googly of perfect length which beat his forward push and bowled him through the gate.

Eyewitnesses stated that both Bill O'Reilly and Jack Fingleton, who were reporting on the match for their Australian newspapers, were so hysterically happy at Bradman's misfortune – which, of course, led to his final Test average falling just under the coveted 100 mark – that it became somewhat embarrassing for the box's other occupants. Both O'Reilly and Fingleton hardly disguised their lifelong antipathy towards aspects of Bradman's personality and his alleged selfishness when it came to many of his own playing performances, but that they felt so strongly as to revel in his great anti-climactic farewell innings is quite another thing.

Bradman, who had walked to the wicket in the last Test of the 1948 series needing just four runs to be sure of averaging the magic 100 in his international career, found himself forever linked with the frustrating (but still barely believable) Test average of 99.94 as a result of his dramatic duck. It is a part of cricket folklore that he was beaten and bowled because he still had a tear or two in his eyes following his emotional reception. No doubt O'Reilly and Fingleton would have laughed aloud at that little tale, too. The Don, it is readily confirmed by most who knew him, would never have allowed himself to become misty-eyed at the crease if there were runs to be made.

Was Bradman, though, the most cold-hearted and emotionless killer of bowling attacks in cricket history? His incredible career figures suggest he was, although contemporaries insist that Hammond could have finished with similar figures if he had married his matchless talent with the Don's ferocious concentration and dedication to scoring literally as many runs as possible.

Bradman's average in all Ashes competition was 89.78, and his 30 Test innings in England came at an average of 102.84. Eight of his nineteen Test hundreds against England were converted into double centuries; two of those were in turn translated into triples. In all first-class cricket in England, on his four Ashes tours, Bradman amassed 41 hundreds (and twelve scores of more than 200) from 120 innings – at an average of 96.44. And, after that Oval Test duck, he went on to score 150, 143 and 153 in his last three innings on English soil. Purely in terms of the business of run-getting, the man was simply insatiable and world cricket has never seen anyone else like him.

1950–51

TWO DECLARATIONS ON A BRISBANE 'STICKY'

The opening Test of the 1950–51 series provided one of the most remarkable-looking scorecards in the history of the international game. Just one glance and you know something was afoot . . . and the culprit was the all too familiar Brisbane 'sticky dog'. And, unfortunately for England, at the start of a rubber in which they suffered rough luck throughout, Freddie Brown's team were on the wrong end of it.

England initially enjoyed the best of starts when the Ashes battle began on 1 December 1950. Australia, playing in a series against England without the presence of Bradman for the first time since 1926, batted poorly on a fine surface and were dismissed for just 228. Then it rained. Play did not resume until 1 p.m. on the third day, and by then the conditions had been severely altered. In a short calm before the storm, England openers Cyril Washbrook and Reg Simpson put on 28. Then came cricketing carnage, with 20 wickets falling in the last two sessions of the shortened day: by the close, England were 30 for 6 . . . in their second innings.

England, first time around, had collapsed from 49 for 1 to 67 for 7 as the pitch became ever more spiteful. The sublime skills of Len Hutton, coming in at number six in an allegedly tactical bid to stiffen the sinews of the middle order, went largely wasted as he was only on 8 not out when Brown decided to cut his losses and declare England's first innings closed at 68 for 7. Australia, now themselves caught in impossible conditions, reacted by declaring their own second

111

innings when it was already in ruins at 32 for 7 – setting a target of 193.

This left England with just over an hour's batting in what remained of an already remarkable day. But, now, even with a succession of lower middle-order players being sent in to try to see out time and protect the front-line batsmen, they saw their Test hopes all but disappear. By the close, they had lost six wickets – with Arthur McIntyre capping a disastrous day by getting himself run out attempting a fourth run.

Hutton, now in at eight to join Godfrey Evans, was England's last hope on a pitch that had, by the following morning, at last dried out. But, at 46, Bill Johnston followed up his first innings 5 for 35 by dismissing both Evans and Denis Compton, in at nine, with successive balls. From 46 for 8, Hutton's reaction was both savage and supreme: jumping down the pitch to the spinners, and also attacking the faster bowlers with thrilling strokes, Hutton simply went for it. Sadly, he lost Brown at 77, but with last man Doug Wright hanging on at the other end, the Yorkshireman destined to become England's first professional captain kept up his defiant assault. Eventually, when Wright holed out off a Jack Iverson long hop, Hutton was 62 not out and England, all out for 122, had lost by 70 runs.

In the tense, low-scoring second Test, which began on 22 December and featured two successive rest days on 24 December, a Sunday, and Christmas Day, Hutton was the first-innings victim of what England were convinced was an appalling umpiring decision. In the end, needing 179 to square the series, they were bowled out for 150 to lose by a mere 28 runs.

At 2–0 down, England's luck needed to change, but didn't. The third Test was lost by an innings and thirteen runs, with both Trevor Bailey and leg-spinner Wright being unable to bowl at all in the match after suffering injury during England's first innings of 290. Bailey had his thumb broken by a ball from Ray Lindwall and Wright tore a tendon in his leg in the act of being run out for 0. Compton's second-innings 23 was his highest score in a wretched series in which he totalled just 53 runs at an average of 7.57, but at least England pulled back to 4–1 at the end by winning the fifth Test back in Melbourne (their first post-war victory over Australia) by eight wickets.

Hutton scored, in total, 532 runs at 88.83 and an equally heroic Alec Bedser took 30 wickets at 16.06, while in that final Test Simpson's brilliant unbeaten 156 on his 31st birthday, and his 74-run last-wicket stand with Roy Tattersall, also proved vital. Hopes of a better future for England still flickered.

JIM BURKE: GLORIOUS BEGINNING, BITTER END

It was on the morning of 2 February 1979 that Jim Burke – still aged only 48 – walked into a Sydney store and bought himself a gun. That afternoon, he used it to take his own life.

Exactly 28 years earlier, on 2 February 1951, Burke had made his debut for Australia when he was selected for the fourth Test of the 1950–51 Ashes series. Australia won by 274 runs, and on the fifth day of the game Burke – at the age of 20 years and 240 days – marked his first appearance for his country by scoring an unbeaten 101 from number six.

He went on to play in 24 Tests, also featuring strongly in both the 1956 and 1958–59 Ashes series and hitting another two Test hundreds. Burke looked what he was: determined, nuggety, with his cap reportedly worn tugged down over one eye, further shading his face. He was dark-haired and had a prominent jaw which merely added to his pugnacious character. As an opener in the Brisbane Test of 1958–59 he scored 28 not out in 250 minutes as Australia made 147 from 51.7 eight-ball overs to win the match by eight wickets. Even his three Test hundreds could best be described as unexciting to watch, but he was a mightily effective opening batsman who formed with Colin McDonald an enduring and successful opening partnership for Australia. In a first-class career which stretched from 1948 to 1959, he scored 7,563 runs overall at the healthy average of 45.01.

In middle age, and with his cricket career already in the distant past, he suffered personal and financial worries, and was also trying to face up to a major hip operation which he feared was going to prevent him from playing his beloved regular rounds of golf. His suicide, however, came as a considerable shock to friends of the man who, for Australia and New South Wales, had shown such strength of character at the crease.

1953

THE CHAIRMAN OF SELECTORS WHO PICKED HIMSELF

Freddie Brown was a wholehearted, and indeed big-hearted, all-round cricketer who made his Test debut in 1931 and was a member of Douglas Jardine's 1932–33 England squad in Australia. Ruddy-faced and jolly, and born in the Peruvian capital of Lima, he was a larger than life character who captained England in the 1950–51 Ashes series, and also in the home rubbers against the West Indies in 1950 and South Africa in 1951. By 1953, though, he was 42 years old and very much in the autumn of his county career with a Northamptonshire side that he had rejuvenated following his move from Surrey. He was also chairman of England's selectors.

After the opening Test of 1953 had been drawn at Trent Bridge, with Alec Bedser's fourteen wickets setting up what might have been an England win but for the rain which cut off their quest to score a last-innings 229 at 120 for 1, Brown was persuaded by his fellow selectors to make a playing comeback himself at the second Test at Lord's. He did not disgrace himself, either, taking four second-innings Australian wickets for 82 and scoring 22 and 28 at number seven in a revamped English batting order.

Yet Brown's romantic single-match comeback, after two years out of Test cricket, was rather dwarfed in significance by one of the most remarkable and celebrated rearguard actions seen in the Test arena. England looked destined for defeat when they slipped to 73 for 4 in their second innings, after finding themselves needing 343 to win, with almost five hours of the match left to play. Enter Trevor Bailey, the Essex all-rounder, to join Willie Watson in a partnership which captured the attention of the whole nation.

The five-match series, as a whole, attracted a new record aggregate attendance of 549,650 people, but there were literally millions glued to their radios on that last day of Coronation month, June 1953, to check that Watson and Bailey were still there. And, for a shade over four and a quarter hours, in a stand worth 163 runs which lasted from 12.42 p.m. to 5.50 p.m. – just 40 minutes before the scheduled close of the match – they were. Bailey finally fell for 71, made in 257 minutes, while Watson marked his debut against Australia by hitting 109 and defying their bowlers for 346 minutes.

England's magnificent draw, clinched at 282 for 7, kept the Ashes dream alive . . . and put cricket way out on its own at the head of the summer's sporting agenda at the end of a month which had begun (on 2 June) with the coronation of Queen Elizabeth II in Westminster Abbey and the conquest of Mount Everest by Edmund Hillary and Sherpa Tensing.

THE SMALL BOY IN THE OVAL CROWD

After narrow squeaks for both sides – Australia collapsed to a startling 35 for 8 in the little time rain allowed for their second innings in the third Test at Old Trafford, but England's bowlers then had to resort to negative tactics to leave the Australians a mere 30 runs short of a win target of 177 in 115 minutes at the end of the fourth Test at Headingley – the 1953 series decider was won by England, to the unbridled joy of a nation.

Brian Johnston's memorable television commentary – 'The Ashes! It's the Ashes!' – as Denis Compton swept the winning boundary down to the Oval gasholders, giving England their comprehensive eight-wicket win and 1–0 series triumph, is rightly replayed time and again. To English minds, the winning back of the Ashes in Coronation year – and, moreover, after a then record barren period without them of 18 years and 362 days – remains a sporting moment as golden and treasured as they come.

The truly special way the long and dramatic history of the Ashes story has caught the imagination of so many successive generations, however, is perhaps best illustrated by the little-known tale of how one particular wide pair of fourteen-year-old eyes came to be watching spellbound from beside the Oval boundary on that never-to-be-forgotten day.

Brian Luckhurst, who nineteen years later as a stalwart of the great Kent team of the 1970s was destined himself to hit the Ashes-clinching runs in a Test for England, had travelled by train from his home in north Kent to see history, he hoped, being made. What is more, the young Luckhurst had come up to London's Victoria Station the evening before, with a school mate for company, and the pair had walked to the Oval before eating their packed meals and – together with hundreds more who were frightened that they might not get in the next day – settling themselves down to sleep the night outside the ground.

They, and thousands more, were not disappointed on that particular 19 August. England's victory arrived just before 3 p.m. on the fourth afternoon of a match scheduled to run over six days.

At that time a cricket-mad kid fired still further by what he had witnessed, Luckhurst was to cap a long career in county cricket by winning his first international cap at the age of 31. He played in three Ashes series in the early 1970s and was also a part of another England team – in 1970–71 – that experienced the exhilaration of winning back the Ashes after long years without them.

1954–55

ENGLAND'S EMBARRASSMENT OF RICHES

The wonder of the team that England selected to hold on to the Ashes in 1954–55 was as much in who was left out of the tour party as in who was chosen.

Has a more powerful and more balanced England bowling attack ever been sent overseas? That Ashes series was won, of course, by the pace of Frank Tyson – supported by Brian Statham, Trevor Bailey, and the twin spin threat of Bob Appleyard and Johnny Wardle.

Alec Bedser, after playing in the opening Test at Brisbane – which England lost disastrously after skipper Len Hutton had put Australia in – was then dropped and never played in another Ashes Test. But just look at the bowlers England also left at home: Fred Trueman for one, plus the spinners Jim Laker, Tony Lock and Roy Tattersall.

Hutton, however, made grave errors of tactical and selectorial judgement in that opening Test, before the typhoon that was Tyson began to blow. At Brisbane the Australians racked up a massive 601 for 8 declared after Hutton had sent them in, with England having chosen no slow bowler in their four-man attack for only the second time in their history. To make matters worse, Denis Compton then broke a finger in his left hand when he trapped it in the pickets during England's leather-chasing on the first two days. Compton was only able to bat at the end of the order, making 2 not out and 0 as England were dismissed for 190 and 257 to lose by an innings and 154 runs.

The transformation, however, was complete when England won the next three Tests to make Hutton the first English captain to regain and then retain the Ashes. Bowling as fast off a shortened run as any man has ever done, Tyson took 25 Australian scalps in those three Tests – with Statham bagging thirteen and Appleyard ten.

Tyson had begun the tour with the long run-up (40 to 50 yards) he used in England. Strongly built, but of average height, he did not have the most fluent of actions, and he put enormous strain on his body with a big final delivery stride, which led to a catalogue of injuries during his comparatively short top-flight career. On the advice of his colleagues, and following the battering he and the other bowlers took in the lost first Test of the series, he found he could work up much the same pace off a much-shortened run, and that this also helped his accuracy and enabled him to bowl faster for longer.

Tyson, moreover, had been knocked unconscious, struck on the back of the head by a Ray Lindwall bouncer from which he turned away as he ducked, during England's second innings of the pivotal second Test at Sydney. Initial reports were that he would play no further part in the match; they were wrong. Tyson not only reappeared to continue his innings (which ended when he was bowled by Lindwall for 9) but then took 6 for 85 as Australia were bowled out for 184 to lose by 38 runs.

England's two last-wicket stands in this tough, tight match were 43 between Wardle and Statham, and then 46 between Appleyard and Statham. By such slender threads hangs the fate of nations.

1956

LAKER SCALES MOUNT OLYMPUS

What was it like, at Old Trafford on 31 July 1956, to be Tony Lock? The left-arm spinner had just seen his Surrey and England colleague Jim Laker take all ten Australian second-innings wickets to make sure the Ashes stayed in England . . . after Laker had already taken 9 for 37 in the Aussies' first innings!

Lock's solitary success in this amazing match came when he took the third Australian wicket in their first-innings collapse to 84 all out, having opener Jim Burke caught by Colin Cowdrey off his glove. From then on, he was but a mere foil to Laker's subtle thrusts.

From around the wicket, Laker demonstrated a mastery of flight and accuracy and spin to earn himself cricketing immortality. Conditions in the match were not that of a 'bunsen burner' – the pitch was a bit dusty, said contemporary reports, but there was nothing untoward in terms of how the ball behaved. The respective figures of Laker and Lock from that fourth Ashes Test make for remarkable reading: in the first innings Laker's were 16.4–4–37–9, and Lock's 14–3–37–1; in the second Laker's were 51.2–23–53–10 and Lock's a scarcely believable 55–30–69–0.

In Australia's first innings Laker removed seven Australian batsmen for just eight runs in the space of 22 balls, but the second-innings miracle was a far more drawn-out affair, with Colin McDonald in particular batting defiantly for Australia to score 89. England's other bowlers sent down just ten overs in the Australian first innings (Statham bowling six overs, Bailey four), but 44 in the second innings (Statham bowled sixteen, Bailey 20, Alan Oakman eight). Laker bowled the tenth over of the first innings, and came on after just 20 minutes in Australia's second innings – at 20 for no wicket. Lock, meanwhile, apparently lost his length in the second innings, which may partly account for his lack of success. All Laker's nineteen wickets were taken from the Stretford End, and by the end of the series – which England won 2–1 – he had earned himself a record Ashes haul of 46 wickets.

Yet, perhaps the most incredible aspect of the 1956 summer is that Laker did not just take all ten wickets in an innings against the Australians once; no, playing for Surrey earlier in the tour, off-spinner Laker had single-handedly bowled out the Aussies for 259 at the Oval with an analysis of 46–18–88–10. Lock, this time, at least had the consolation of taking a second-innings 7 for 49 himself as Surrey became the first English county to beat the Australians since 1912.

And, as a postscript to Laker's unique double of ten-wicket hauls in 1956, before this amazing summer was out Lock had also earned himself an innings maximum: playing for Surrey against Kent at Blackheath, he took 10 for 54. You simply could not make it up!

1958–59

BAILEY'S FINEST SEVEN AND A HALF HOURS

In the opening Test of the 1958–59 Ashes series, at Brisbane, Trevor Bailey scored 68 runs from 40 scoring strokes: four fours, three threes, ten twos and 23 singles. Unfortunately for spectators, and also for viewers in what was the first Test match in Australia to be televised live, Bailey also faced another 385 deliveries from which he failed to score. The main image of his innings was the forward defensive prod – repeated ad nauseam.

His 68 took him, in all, 458 minutes – after he had rattled past 50 in a shade under six hours. Throughout his innings, the only half-century of a bizarre match in which almost everyone found run scoring a tortuous process until the debutant, Norman O'Neill, blazed to 71 not out to win the game on the fifth day, Bailey crept along at an average of slightly less than nine runs per hour.

TV viewers would surely have nodded off in their thousands. Besides Bailey, the rest of the entertainment (O'Neill at the end excepted) was utterly tedious too: England's first-innings total of 134 took the entire opening day, Australia replied on day two with 156 for 6, and then came two more days in which the Australians reached 186 all out and England – with Bailey to the fore – crawled to a second-innings 198. Indeed, the fourth day produced a mere 106 runs as England lost their last eight wickets and almost ground to a complete halt after beginning the day on 92 for 2. A total of just 518 runs from the first four days made this the strangest opening salvo (more of an opening yawn?) of any Ashes series.

Australia won by eight wickets, however, to kick off a series in which they would regain the Ashes by slaughtering 4–0 an England side which, on paper, looked as formidable as it had ever been with Peter May, Colin Cowdrey and Tom Graveney to anchor the batting and a bowling attack boasting the pace of Tyson, Trueman, Statham and Peter Loader and the spin of Laker and Lock.

Bailey, the all-round pivot of the England side for a decade, played in all five Tests of his final series but whether he should have been used by skipper May at the head of the England order (especially with May himself and Cowdrey often appearing inexplicably at numbers five and six) is open to question. Tyson's typhoon had blown itself out, robbing them of their obvious spearhead, but England seemed to allow Australia to set the agenda right from the start of the series. Bailey marked his 61st and final Test with a pair at Melbourne, meanwhile, beaten in both innings by a new ball propelled by Ray Lindwall.

Bailey's bowling and fielding were always exemplary but his twelve biggest innings against Australia, spread over five Ashes series, saw him total 345 runs in a combined crease occupation of 31 hours and 20 minutes. In other words, even when he got himself 'in', the man who in later life, as a much-respected summariser with the BBC's *Test Match Special* radio commentary team, was always referred to as 'The Boil', scored his runs at the miserly rate of eleven per hour.

1961

SUBBA ROW MAINTAINS ENGLAND'S 'INDIAN SIGN'

Raman Subba Row went on to become a much-respected chairman of the Test and County Cricket Board, from 1985 to 1990, and he has also served on various Lord's committees and for Surrey as club chairman. But it was as an England opening batsman in the 1961 series that he succeeded in maintaining one of the more remarkable sequences in Ashes history. The fourth batsman of Indian extraction to represent England, though born in London, Subba Row followed in the tradition of Ranjitsinhji, Duleepsinhji and the Nawab of Pataudi in making a century in his first Test innings against Australia.

Curiously, the fifth player in this line – Nasser Hussain – almost kept up the sequence by making 71 at Trent Bridge against the 1993 Australians.

Subba Row, meanwhile, also had the distinction of scoring a further hundred in his final Test innings against Australia, in the fifth Test of a 1961 series which the Australians won 2–1 to retain the Ashes. His 112 at Edgbaston and 137 at the Oval (98 runs of which were scored with a runner after pulling a leg muscle) helped Subba Row to top England's batting averages for the series, with 468 runs at an average of 46.80. And yet, a month after his highest Test innings, and third century in thirteen England appearances, Subba Row announced he was retiring from the first-class game for business reasons. He was still only 29, had captained Northamptonshire for the previous four seasons, had a Test average of 46.85 and a first-class one of 41.46, and might have been a strong candidate to lead his country at some stage if he had stayed in the game.

What is more, Peter May, who had captained England for a then record 41 times and won 66 caps, also announced his retirement after this final Test of 1961 – again, at the premature age of 31. Strangely, too, a third regular member of England's top order in that Ashes series – Ted Dexter – was to give up international cricket at 30 in 1965, although he did at least come out of retirement for two more Tests against the Australians of 1968 before taking his final leave of the highest stage.

1962–63

ENGLAND'S MISSIONARY TO AUSTRALIA

The England team which travelled to Australia by air and sea for the 1962–63 series included the first ordained minister to play Test cricket. Indeed, the Reverend David Sheppard was required to take sabbatical leave from his missionary work at the Mayflower Centre in London's East End in order to answer England's call.

Sheppard, then 33, had begun his Test career twelve years earlier in 1950 and, in 1954, had actually led England in two Test matches against Pakistan. Ordained in 1955, he scored the second of his three Test hundreds when recalled towards the end of the 1956 Ashes series, but his Church of England ministry work then began to restrict the amount of first-class cricket he could play for his county, Sussex.

Recalled by England's selectors with success, however, for the last two Tests of the 1962 series against Pakistan, Sheppard was then asked to make himself available for the following winter's Ashes tour. Taking his sabbatical winter in order to play Test cricket again, he also took advantage of the opportunity to preach in Australian churches throughout the team's progress from state to state. And, in the second Test at Melbourne, he found proper reward for his devotion to the cause by completing his final century for England. He would have had the satisfaction of hitting the winning single, too, but was run out for 113 attempting it.

During England's seven-wicket win, which was enough to secure a 1–1 series draw but not – alas – to bring back the

Ashes, Sheppard had earlier made a duck and dropped two catches. This had prompted the sometimes irreverent fast bowler Fred Trueman, Yorkshire's pride, to make the memorable but affectionate quip: 'It's a pity Reverend don't put his hands together more often in t'field!'

Sheppard's first-class career ended in 1963, after three more Test appearances in New Zealand at the end of that same tour had taken his number of England caps to 22, and he rose to become Bishop of Woolwich before his further elevation to the post of Bishop of Liverpool in 1975.

1964

WHEN AUSTRALIA WERE HAPPY WITH THE DULLEST OF DRAWS

In an Ashes Test, do you always set out to win the game? What is more important: winning the game, or winning the Ashes series? In the fourth Test of the 1964 series, at Old Trafford, Australian captain Bobby Simpson was in no doubt.

His team had just gone 1–0 up in the series, after winning a Leeds Test which turned on England skipper Ted Dexter's fateful decision to remove his spinners, Fred Titmus and Norman Gifford, from the attack when they had already reduced Australia to 178 for 7 in their first innings, still 90 runs in arrears. Dexter, believing that it was pace that would blow away the Australian tail, took the new ball and handed it to Fred Trueman and Jack Flavell. In truth, they did not bowl terribly well, but it was also just the sort of challenge that Peter Burge, the one remaining front-line batsman, loved.

Far happier against the quicks than the slows, Burge cut and pulled his way from 38 to a career-defining 160. Neil Hawke and Wally Grout both hit 37 at the other end to help him add 105 and 89 for the eighth and ninth wickets respectively, and Australia were suddenly in an ascendancy which led, in turn, to a seven-wicket victory.

As holders of the Ashes, Simpson knew that Australia needed just to draw the Manchester Test which began a fortnight later. Winning the toss and going in first himself, with Bill Lawry, Simpson set out to clinch the Ashes and then – and only then – consider what else might be done.

He played safe to the tune of batting on until a declaration at 12.30 on the third day – by which time Australia's total was 656 for 8. Simpson and Lawry had begun the establishment of this impregnable position by putting on 201 for the first wicket, and Simpson led so effectively from the front that he not only made his maiden Test hundred, in his 52nd innings, but went on to score an epic 311 in twelve hours and 42 minutes at the crease.

England's Tom Cartwright bowled 77 overs of controlled medium pace, but Australian off-spinner Tom Veivers topped even that show of stamina when Dexter's team – with nothing to gain other than to bat out time themselves – replied by grinding their way to 611. Veivers bowled 95.1 overs – 36 of them maidens, to Cartwright's 32 – and returned figures of 3 for 155 in comparison to the England man's 2 for 118. Ken Barrington, with 256, added 246 for the third wicket with Dexter, who made 174 before being bowled by Veivers. There was then just time, on the fall of England's tenth wicket, for Lawry and Simpson to face two overs, bowled by Titmus and Barrington, before the match ended in the draw that confirmed Australia as continued holders of the coveted urn.

Simpson's tactics were justified by that fact, to some, but others wondered if it was right for a sporting spectacle to play second fiddle to the mythical Ashes prize . . . especially when there was still one more Test to be played in the series. And that Test, too, was to end in a draw.

1965–66

THE DAY THAT BARBER WAS A CUT ABOVE

One of the great mysteries of sport is how, on one particular day, any given player can perform way above his 'normal' capacity. Suddenly, it is as if he has been touched by the gods, but then equally swiftly comes the return to mere mortality.

Such a day for Bob Barber – top-order batsman and useful leg-spinner – arrived on 7 January 1966, when he lit up the Sydney Cricket Ground with a quite glorious innings of 185 in just under five hours.

Barber, a tall left-hander who went for his strokes, never bettered this score in a first-class career spanning sixteen years, and it remained his only Test century even though he played for England on no fewer than 28 occasions. Yet, on this day of days, he was utterly in charge against an Australian attack that simply could not contain him; after reaching his hundred in 198 minutes, he powered on to strike nineteen fours in his 255-ball masterpiece. He dominated an opening partnership of 234 in 242 minutes with Geoff Boycott and, with John Edrich also scoring a century, England were able to reach a position from which they eventually forced an innings victory.

Barber's great innings might even have inspired Ashes glory, too, but England could not hold on to the 1–0 lead they had gained from this third-Test victory – losing the next match, at Adelaide, by an innings and nine runs. Barber made a duck and 19.

After bringing his first-class career prematurely to a close in 1969, just before turning 34, Barber concentrated on a business career that was to make him a wealthy man. He ran a company that manufactured and sold hygienic blue water-colourants for lavatory cisterns. And, outside of the business world, he also revealed the natural freedom and adventurous-ness of his spirit by joining, aged 45 in 1980, a tough mountaineering expedition in the Himalayas.

1968

'DEADLY' MOPS UP

In a moment that has been immortalised by one of cricket's most famous photographs, Derek Underwood traps Australian opener John Inverarity lbw for a skilled and stubborn 56 – made after 250 minutes of resistance – and England have won the 1968 Oval Test by 226 runs in the most dramatic of circumstances, with only five minutes to spare. A split second after Inverarity has been beaten by Underwood's arm ball, all eleven England players circling the Australian are caught on camera as they join in the successful appeal.

The 23-year-old Underwood's 7 for 50 reinforced his growing reputation as a 'deadly' performer on a rain-affected pitch; indeed, the great Kent left-arm spinner still answers to that nickname today. Yet this memorable and iconic moment for a bowler who was to end up with 297 Test wickets was only able to happen because of the extraordinary reaction of an Oval crowd totally determined that, if at all possible, Australia should not be allowed to be saved by a rainstorm.

England, having been in command ever since John Edrich and Basil D'Oliveira both made big first-innings hundreds, looked like wrapping up the match in some comfort as Australia collapsed to 86 for 5 in their second innings, with Underwood grabbing three of the wickets to fall. But then, on the stroke of lunch, rain began to fall and drove the players off a minute before the scheduled interval.

In the next half hour a freak storm developed, flooding almost the entire playing area and seeming to make an

abandonment the only likely outcome. The spectators, however, were having none of it as, just as suddenly, the sun
reappeared.

Groundstaff from the Surrey club supervised an heroic
mopping-up effort, which involved hundreds of volunteers
from the crowd, both young and old. Mostly carrying brooms
or blankets, they waded out into the vast puddles of casual
water covering the outfield and either brushed it away to the
boundary edge or, by the use of vigorous spiking, persuaded it
to disappear underground. Any remaining surface water was
soaked up by the blankets, laid on the turf.

Eventually, at 4.45 p.m., and with the pitch surrounds
heavily sawdusted, play restarted. At first, Inverarity and Barry
Jarman, the Aussie wicket-keeper, seemed more than capable
of saving the game. But, after D'Oliveira bowled Jarman for 21
with the clock showing 5.24 p.m., great excitement filled the
Oval stands. Underwood, reintroduced immediately at the
Pavilion End by England captain Colin Cowdrey, removed
Ashley Mallett and Graham McKenzie with the first and sixth
deliveries of this decisive spell. John Gleeson, the number ten,
was bowled by Underwood at 5.48 p.m. . . . and Inverarity
finally fell seven minutes later amid the highest tension.

England had squared the series at 1–1, and even the
disappointment that Australia still held the Ashes was forgotten
in all the drama. Sportsmen often say that it is a crowd's
support which makes the difference between success and
failure. In this instance, it was truly the case.

1970–71

THE AUSSIE UMPIRES WHO DIDN'T LIFT A FINGER!

There were no lbw decisions at all given against Australia's batsmen in any of the six Tests which made up the fiercely fought 1970–71 series. As England's players on that tour said afterwards, it must have been just a coincidence!

Now, there is certainly no suggestion of charges of home bias against the three Australian umpires who stood in that series, which England under Ray Illingworth eventually won 2–0 to regain the Ashes after a gap of twelve years. But it remains a curious statistic, one which merely serves to underline how hard Illingworth's team had to battle to earn their ultimate sweet reward of becoming only the fourth English side to win back the Ashes on Australian soil.

And how sweet it was! The destiny of the Ashes even came down to the result of a seventh Test, following the complete abandonment of the scheduled third Test at Melbourne due to prolonged bad weather and the controversial decision to replace it with a hastily arranged match at the same ground (which became the fifth Test) a fortnight later.

They may have been 1–0 up because of their fourth-Test victory, but England knew that this extra game (which, to be fair to the Australians, enabled the rubber still to be contested over its original six-Test distance) gave the Aussies a further chance to square the series and thus keep the Ashes. But, when the (renamed) fifth and sixth Tests were drawn, it all came down to the final match in

134

Sydney. England, without the injured Boycott, were immediately put under extreme pressure when bowled out for just 184 after being put in by new Australian captain Ian Chappell.

A solid bowling performance could not prevent Australia from gaining an 80-run first innings lead, and it took a determined opening partnership of 94 between John Edrich and Brian Luckhurst, who both scored fifties, to renew English hopes. There had been much drama and no little controversy late on the second day when fast bowler John Snow, England's magnificent spearhead, struck Terry Jenner on the head with a short-pitched ball. That led to severe crowd disturbances, with missiles being thrown on to the outfield, and Illingworth reacted by leading his team from the field. Only when all hurled objects had been cleared away did England return.

England's subsequent progress to 302 all out in their second innings meant that Australia needed to score 223, with two and a half days of the scheduled six-day allocation still left. Snow, having bowled opener Ken Eastwood for 0, then fractured and dislocated his right little finger when he collided with the boundary pickets trying to catch a hook by Keith Stackpole. Snow needed hospital treatment and could not bowl again in the match, but five other England bowlers also got wickets, led by Illingworth's 3 for 39 from 20 overs, and by 12.36 p.m. on the fifth day the Ashes were England's as Australia were bowled out for 160.

Illingworth was chaired from the field by his triumphant team and a celebratory lunchtime party was soon being started up inside the England dressing room. Later that night, at a private dinner with friends, Basil D'Oliveira was still so jubilant (and so 'emotional') that he apparently kept on saying – to whomever would listen – 'We stuffed the bastards' over and over again.

Then, when the England team flew out of Australia to New Zealand, for a three-Test series against the Kiwis, the pilot of the Air New Zealand flight made an announcement to welcome

135

Illingworth's squad on board, adding: 'And well done for beating Australia!' The balance of Ashes power had again tipped England's way at last.

1972

THE COUNTY REJECT WHO ROUTED ENGLAND

In 1970 a hopeful young swing bowler from Western Australia was offered a two-match trial by Northamptonshire on the strength of some good performances in the Scottish League, where he was playing in a bid to widen his experience. In those two games, for Northants Second XI, Bob Massie had overall figures of 3 for 166. He was not offered even a short-term county contract.

Two years later, mainly as a result of taking 6 for 27 for an Australian XI against the Rest of the World in Sydney, he was chosen for the 1972 Ashes squad. Making his debut at Lord's, in the second Test, the 25-year-old Massie swung the ball so prodigiously that he took 8 for 84 in England's first innings, and then a further 8 for 53 in their second. Australia, not surprisingly, won by eight wickets. Massie was often as unplayable as any bowler can ever have been – swinging the ball prodigiously both ways from around the wicket in a sticky and humid atmosphere. Only Brian Luckhurst, who fell twice to Dennis Lillee, escaped Massie's clutches.

He bowled excellently, too, in the next Test at Trent Bridge, picking up four English scalps in the first innings and five in total, but then only two more wickets in the last two Tests of a rubber which was drawn 2–2. England, who had won the fourth Test at Headingley to take an unbeatable 2–1 lead, with Derek Underwood taking ten wickets in the match on a grassless, diseased pitch, retained the Ashes.

The following Australian season saw Massie take another eight wickets in two Tests against Pakistan, but although he toured West Indies in early 1973, and played in six first-class games with moderate results, he found he could never swing the ball as much as he did at Lord's on his astonishing debut.

The Test career of Robert Arnold Lockyer Massie was over, and he also lost his place in his state side in the 1973–74 season. Indeed, he took only 179 wickets in a first-class career which stretched from 1965 to 1975, leaving 'Massie's Test' at Lord's in 1972 as one of the great oddities in Test match cricket history. The match figures of 16 for 137 achieved by the previously unknown bowler from Perth may stand for many a long year as the record haul for a Test debutant.

When his playing days were over, Massie became a regular commentator on Test cricket for ABC radio in Australia, but it is as the meteor which scorched the hallowed turf of Lord's that he will be forever remembered.

1974–75

VETERAN COWDREY HAS 'A LOT OF FUN'

Chris Cowdrey often tells the story of when his father Colin received the call from England's selectors to fly out to join England's 1974–75 Ashes tour as an emergency replacement, following the hand fractures suffered by both Dennis Amiss and John Edrich in the opening Test at Brisbane. Dennis Lillee, who himself was fast enough, had just been joined by the terrifying catapult-style pace of Jeff Thomson in Australia's new-ball attack . . . and the pair had shared thirteen wickets as England had been overwhelmed by 166 runs in the first Test.

'Why on earth are you going, Dad?' asked young Chris, then seventeen and already a highly promising young cricketer himself. 'Well, it might be a lot of fun!' replied Colin, then less than a month short of his 42nd birthday.

Cowdrey senior had not appeared in a Test since June 1971; now he was about to fly out of the depths of an English winter to join up with Mike Denness's shell-shocked troops in Perth. Amazingly, too, just four days after his flight touched down on Australian soil, Cowdrey was walking out to bat at number three in the second Test. A packed crowd at the WACA ground gave the venerable former England captain a tremendous reception . . . and yet they looked on with an almost ghoulish fascination. Did Cowdrey know what he was doing? Did he know just how fast Thomson and Lillee were, especially here at Perth on one of the quickest pitches in the world?

Those who were there swear that the rotund and genteel Englishman, soon after reaching the middle, offered his hand to Thomson by way of greeting. 'Hello, I don't believe we've met. My name's Cowdrey.' Thommo's reply is not as well recorded, although open-mouthed astonishment is the most likely initial reaction.

That Cowdrey survived the ensuing onslaught at all, let alone scored 22 and 41 (opening the batting in the second innings!) in the match, is a tribute both to his courage and technique. In 1974–75, remember, as Lillee and Thomson swept Australia to the Ashes with three wins in the first four Tests, batsmen still did not wear helmets, arm guards or chest-protectors.

1975

THE BANK CLERK WHO MARCHED
OUT TO WAR

If there ever was an Ashes tale to capture a wider imagination even than that of the vast sporting public of England and Australia, it occurred at Lord's on the last day of July 1975. And yet David Steele, the grey-haired and bespectacled 33-year-old journeyman county batsman who won the hearts of a nation for the way he stood up to the twin terrors of Lillee and Thomson when they were threatening to plunge England into cricketing oblivion, almost didn't even find his way out into the middle.

Leaving the unfamiliar 'home' dressing room at Lord's to walk down the stairs and out through the pavilion's famous Long Room, Steele was so emotionally caught up in the moment – and the overwhelming need to keep his eyes averted from well-wishers and compose himself for the challenge that awaited him – that he went down one flight of stairs too many and found himself outside the gentlemen's lavatories.

Suddenly realising his mistake, Steele rushed back up the steps and – eventually – emerged blinking into the sunlight to face a situation in which England, already 1–0 down after being crushed by Australia in the opening Test at Edgbaston, and with a new captain in Tony Greig following Mike Denness' subsequent resignation, were rocking again at 10 for 1. Soon, too, the scoreboard read 49 for 4 with Dennis Lillee having swept aside Barry Wood, John Edrich, Dennis Amiss and Graham Gooch.

What followed, though, has already passed into Ashes legend. The unlikely figure of Steele scored the most heroic of half-centuries and helped Greig, who had been instrumental in his shock selection, to put on 96 for the fifth wicket. England, with Greig and Alan Knott then adding 77 and Knott and Bob Woolmer a further 66, recovered to reach 315. English cricket, seemingly lifeless on the floor after the batterings it had taken from Lillee and Jeff Thomson over the previous eight months, suddenly had heroes again – and, as he went through the rest of the series without a single failure, Steele was the biggest hero of all.

He scored 50, 45, 73, 92, 39 and 66 and England drew the Tests at Lord's, Headingley and the Oval. The series was lost 1–0 and the Ashes were still Australia's, but the bleeding had been stopped. Dubbed by one cricket writer as 'looking like a bank clerk going to war' when he marched out for his debut innings at Lord's in England's moment of crisis, Steele also proved his dramatic late entrance into international cricket was no fluke when he took a century off the fearsome West Indies pace attack in 1976, at Trent Bridge.

Steele had made his first-class debut as long ago as 1963 and was, in 1975, organising his Northamptonshire benefit season after a worthy decade and more as a solid, if unspectacular, top-order batsman and a tidy slow left-arm spinner. As part of the support for his county benefit, moreover, Steele's local butcher had promised him and his wife a free meat chop of their choice for every first-class run he scored during the summer. It may have proved a more than generous gesture from the butcher, but by the end of the 1975 season he could not have wished for more or better publicity!

Steele scored 365 runs from his six innings in the 1975 Ashes series, topping England's averages with 60.83 and proving just how effective a tried and tested technique – allied to limitless courage and concentration – could be against even the most ferocious of fast bowling. At the end of the year his benefit had netted him the impressive sum of £25,000 (in addition to several freezers-full of chops) and, in December, he found himself being crowned as BBC Television's Sports Personality of the Year.

1977

BOYCOTT THE CLASSIC HERO AND VILLAIN

Geoff Boycott's triumphant return to Test match cricket in the 1977 Ashes series is a tale of two hundreds, and also provides a classic example of how a sportsman can be a hero and a villain almost simultaneously.

England had gone 1–0 up in the series by winning the second Test at Old Trafford by nine wickets; the 36-year-old Boycott, who had announced before this match that he was available again for international selection after a self-imposed exile of three years, was initially overlooked but then brought back for the third Test at Trent Bridge in place of the out-of-form Dennis Amiss.

This Nottingham Test, by the way, also marked the Test debut of a 21-year-old Ian Botham and featured an eight-minute hold-up of play on the first evening so that both teams could be presented to the Queen and the Duke of Edinburgh on the outfield in front of the pavilion. It was, indeed, the Queen's Silver Jubilee year.

Crowds packed the ground on all five days, and many had come not so much to see the debut of Botham but the return of Boycott and the appearance of local favourite Derek Randall. The popular Nottinghamshire batsman was full of nervous energy, eccentric in a clowning sort of way, and would chatter to anyone on the field; on one occasion, an opposing county team tried to unsettle him by deliberately not talking to him when he came out to bat. He once answered the door of his house wearing batting pads; when asked what he was doing, he replied: 'I'm just breaking them in.' The exact opposite in character to the obsessive, methodical though in his own way equally eccentric Boycott, Randall had scored a brilliant and magical 174 against the Australians in the Centenary Test at Melbourne in March, and had also begun this series with half-centuries in both the first two Tests. Soon, however, in reply to an Australian first-innings total of 243 in which Botham had taken 5 for 74, England had slipped alarmingly to 82 for 5.

There was, moreover, just one major talking point. On 13, and with England on 52 for 2, Randall had been run out by Boycott to leave the Nottingham crowd at first stunned into a shocked silence and then more outspokenly angry at Boycott's part in the dismissal. A notoriously unreliable runner, and with a self-absorption at the crease which many interpreted as selfishness, Boycott had held his head in his hands at the other end after calling his partner for a quick single from a firmish push back up the pitch, only to see the bowler Thomson dart athletically across from his follow-through to seize the ball and run out Randall by yards at the striker's end. So infamous has this incident become to English cricket eyes, in fact, that Nasser Hussain referred to his own mistake of running out Andrew Strauss at Lord's, in what proved to be his final Test innings in 2004, as 'like doing a Boycott on Randall'.

Like Hussain against New Zealand, though, Boycott now steeled himself to do all he could to right the wrong by batting for as long as was possible; and, like Hussain almost 27 years later, he ended up by scoring a hundred as the match was won. With Alan Knott also scoring a magnificent century, the pair added a record 215 for the sixth wicket and gave England a crucial lead of 121.

In the end, after Bob Willis had chipped away at brave Australian second-innings resistance to take 5 for 88, it was Boycott and Randall who were batting together in an unbroken stand of 31 when England completed their seven-wicket victory.

Now, Boycott was cloaked in the hero's mantle once again. His unbeaten second-innings 80 meant (the Randall run-out excepted, of course) a triumphant personal return to the Test arena, and another hundred for Yorkshire in a county match against Warwickshire soon took him to within one of a career tally of 100 first-class centuries. Moreover, the next Test was at Headingley.

And it was almost inevitable that Boycott, the villain image forgotten in front of his own worshipping public, should go on to reach a century at his home ground as, with a technically perfect on-driven boundary, he became the first player in history to go to his 100th hundred in a Test. From 5.49 p.m. on the opening day, play was held up for fully ten minutes as the celebrations in the stands showed no signs of dying and many ecstatic spectators invaded the outfield to congratulate their hero. The Australians, weary with the effort of trying to dislodge the bloody-minded Yorkshireman from the crease, merely sank to the grass. Boycott went on like a true champion to 191 . . . which was 134 runs more than England's next best scorer.

Four days later, meanwhile, after a rest day spent by English cricket people everywhere in delicious anticipation of the Ashes' return, it was a joyous Randall who took the final catch and then turned a cartwheel of celebration. England had regained the Ashes in style with an innings win. Even in Nottingham, Boycott could now be truly forgiven.

1978-79

ENGLAND'S EMBUREY SAVES ASHES RIVAL'S LIFE

Australia, denuded of the majority of their best cricketers by the Kerry Packer schism, lost the 1978–79 Ashes series by a humbling 5–1 margin. In the fifth Test at Adelaide, however, they almost lost one of their opening batsmen too.

Warrick Maxwell Darling, known to all as Rick, had made his Test debut at the end of the previous Australian season, scoring 65 and 56 against India. He had played in the three previous matches against England, reaching 91 in the third Test at Sydney, but now the fair-haired South Australia batsman was to be involved in one of the most frightening accidents ever seen on a cricket field.

England had just been bowled out for 169, with new-found pace ace Rodney Hogg adding another four scalps to his eventual record series total of 41, and Darling – on his home ground – was facing up to Bob Willis's first over with the new ball. Willis's fifth delivery reared up and hit him under the heart with such force that he collapsed on the pitch. Worse, the gum that he was chewing became lodged in his throat. The stricken Darling now lay unconscious and only the quick thinking and actions of John Emburey, one of the nearby English fielders, saved him.

Emburey, the Middlesex off-spinner, revived him by using the first-aid procedure known as the 'pre-cordial thump'. But, even though he was now breathing freely again, Darling remained unconscious and had to be stretchered from the playing arena and brought around in the dressing rooms.

147

Remarkably, however, he was fit enough to resume his innings the following morning, on the fall of the fifth Australian first-innings wicket, but was out to Botham for 15. He was also bowled by England's rising star in the second innings for 18, and his bravery was in another losing cause as Willis and Mike Hendrick mopped up the last Aussie resistance on the fifth day.

1981

THE HERO WHO ALMOST NEVER WAS

Headingley '81 has always been recalled largely as 'Botham's Match', and without the sudden and remarkable renaissance of England's champion all-rounder – who scored 50 and 149 not out and took 6 for 95 in Australia's first innings – the Test would certainly not have entered legend as one of the greatest of all time.

Without Bob Willis, however, on as dramatic a game's final day as the great Ashes story has ever seen, there would have been no happy ending for England . . . and Dennis Lillee and Rodney Marsh, Australia's fast bowler and wicket-keeper respectively, would not have picked up the winnings from a controversial bet after (for a laugh) they put a few pounds on England to win at odds of 500–1 when the home side, in desperate trouble after following on, looked dead and buried.

In fact, the ground bookmakers were unable to pay out the winnings that Lillee and Marsh made from their £10 and £5 bets. The Aussies' bus driver, Peter Tribe, had placed the bets at the Ladbrokes tent and when he went to pick up the money owed there was not enough ready cash left, because so many other canny punters had bet even smaller amounts on the unlikely result. Tribe finally managed to pick up the winning amount (£7,500 in total) at a Ladbrokes betting shop in Worcester, where the Aussies played Worcestershire during the following week. The bookmakers paid out by giving him mainly £5 notes and he arrived in the Australian dressing room with bundles of notes stashed about his person! Lillee and Marsh treated their team-mates to several rounds of drinks with their winnings, and they also paid for Tribe to fly out to Australia for a holiday later in 1981.

But, to return to the fateful last day itself, Willis had been switched to the Kirkstall Lane End after Australia, chasing just 130 for victory, had reached 56 for the loss of just one wicket. He responded with one of the finest and fiercest spells of fast bowling witnessed in a Test arena. His 8 for 43 destroyed Australia, who were bowled out for 111, and England's 18-run victory squared the series at 1–1.

What is not widely known, though, is that Willis was not even in the original team picked by England's selectors for the match, which followed the defeat at Lord's that had cost Ian Botham the captaincy and brought about the return of Mike Brearley as skipper. Willis had suffered from a chest infection during the Lord's Test, and had been ordered to rest up for a week. Mike Hendrick, the Derbyshire seamer, was included in the England XI for Headingley but, before the team was announced publicly, Willis responded to a call from the selectors informing him of their decision by pleading for a chance to prove his fitness.

It was then agreed for Willis to play a day's cricket for his county Warwickshire's second team and, having come through that little test, he was duly given the go-ahead to travel to Leeds and play in the real Test.

Much has been written by cricket historians about whether losing the England captaincy was the weight off his shoulders that inspired Botham to his great deeds of the 1981 series. That will always be a subject of debate. What is beyond dispute is that in the case of Bob Willis, England's other Headingley hero, fate really did lend a hand.

THE STRANGE CASE OF EDGBASTON '81

Everyone remembers the Edgbaston Test of 1981 for the part it played in the wondrous summer-long tale of 'Botham's Ashes'. England's cavalier all-rounder finished a tense, highly charged contest in fairytale fashion, taking five wickets for just one run in the space of 28 balls.

Australia, bowled out in front of a baying, sun-soaked Sunday crowd for 121, having been 105 for 5 when Botham was tossed the ball, had again fallen short of a modest last-innings victory target, and England had – somehow – won the fourth Test of this epic series by 29 runs.

What gripped a country already high on emotion after Headingley was the sheer drama of it all and, of course, Botham's gladiatorial seizure of the moment. What puzzled the professionals, however, after four days of unremittingly tough Test match cricket, was how such a basically sound pitch and a fast outfield baking in hot weather could have produced a low-scoring affair. In all, seventeen batsmen got to 20 – with 25 getting into double figures – but none got to 50. Mike Brearley, the England captain, reached 48 on the first day before edging a wide half-volley from Dennis Lillee to second slip. It remained this odd game's highest individual score.

Mike Gatting's second-innings 39 was England's next best score, while John Emburey's late-order 37 not out, dominating a ninth-wicket stand of 50 with Bob Taylor, was as crucial to England's eventual victory as his match haul of six wickets. For Australia, the top scorers were Kim Hughes (47) and Martin Kent (46) in the first innings and Allan Border (40) in the second.

A brown-coloured pitch did offer consistently low bounce – Lillee kicked the ball away in a show of disgust after bowling the opening over of the match – and it did offer crumbling bowlers' footmarks for rival spinners Emburey and Ray Bright, but essentially it was sound and hardly to blame for totals of 189, 258, 219 and 121.

It was, moreover, the first time in 668 Test matches, going back to West Indies v England on a rain-affected pitch in Bridgetown, Barbados, in January 1935, that no batsman had scored a fifty.

THE TORTOISE AND THE HARE

Ian Botham's miraculous 118 at Old Trafford, in the fifth Test of the 1981 Ashes series, was the innings which finally took all hope away from the Australians, and confirmed England's retention of the precious urn. Eventual victory by 103 runs gave England an unassailable 3–1 lead in the six-match rubber. But while Botham himself reckons his 86-ball hundred was his finest ever, England's champion also believes he could not have done it without the support at the other end of Chris Tavare.

An attractive and often extremely fast-scoring batsman for his county, Kent, Tavare in Test cricket had gained a reputation for slow play to match that of Trevor Bailey. In his defence, however, it must be said that he was frequently asked to provide an anchor role for England, playing as he did among a host of stroke-makers like Gower, Lamb and Botham. He simply carried out his instructions to the letter and with total dedication.

Botham had joined Tavare with England at 104 for 5 in their second innings – a lead of only 205 in improving batting conditions. The Kent batsman had ground out an invaluable near five-hour 69 in England's first innings, and was again playing the anchor role to dogged perfection in a successful return to Test match cricket. This time, Tavare was the calming influence even Botham needed when he arrived at the crease with the whole destination of the Ashes depending largely on the outcome of their sixth-wicket partnership.

At first, Botham matched Tavare's care and caution, with Tavare completing a five-hour half-century (the slowest in a Test in England) and Botham taking 65 minutes and 54 balls to reach an unbeaten 28. The atmosphere was tense, and Botham initially looked to his partner for a lead in the knowledge that he simply had to concentrate on occupying the crease and taking his time to get his eye in.

Then, when Australia took the second new ball, all hell broke loose. Dennis Lillee, who delivered the second over with it, disappeared for 22 as Botham twice hooked him thrillingly for six over long leg off his eyebrows. After scoring just three singles from the first 30 balls he had faced, in 40 minutes, Botham now galloped to his hundred in 104 minutes. In all, his 118 occupied just 102 balls, and he hit six sixes and thirteen fours. His final 97 runs were plundered from only 53 balls faced. When he was out, caught behind by Rod Marsh off Mike Whitney, England's total was 253 and the lead 354. Botham's stand with Tavare had been worth 149, of which Tavare had scored 28.

With Botham gone, Tavare crept on cussedly to 78 – made in two minutes over seven hours at the crease – but the basher was the first to pay tribute afterwards to the blocker. That the Ashes had stayed in England was in large part down to both his and Tavare's contributions, said Botham. For his part, Tavare can afford a smile of satisfaction – even now – for the three runs he earned for on-driving Lillee during that famous new-ball over. Botham had hit the first delivery for six and then had taken a single. Tavare's stroke brought Botham immediately back on strike, and the next two balls disappeared for six and four with the final ball bringing another single.

The tortoise had thus joined the hare in setting a new record for the most runs taken off a Test match over in England and, when Botham had finally blasted his way to his memorable century, Tavare made sure he had his say, as the capacity Old Trafford crowd cheered themselves hoarse. 'Jeez, Beefy, I don't half make you look good!' quipped the lugubrious-looking man of Kent, as Botham accepted his congratulations in mid-pitch.

The destiny of the Ashes was in the balance no more: the dasher and the slowcoach had both reached their objective, at the same time.

1982–83

ALDERMAN'S RUGBY TACKLE INJURY

There have been many rugby-playing cricketers (or vice versa) down the years, and consequently many a cricketer who has suffered injury on the rugby field. But the list of top-class cricketers injured while carrying out a rugby tackle during a cricket match is a very short one: Terry Alderman, during the opening Ashes Test of the 1982–83 series, which took place in mid-November at Perth.

This curious incident occurred near the end of England's slow but secure first-innings progress towards 411; around two dozen spectators, including some England supporters waving a Union Jack flag in celebration of the 400 being reached, took it upon themselves to invade the playing area, and their incursion caused play to be held up. A few then became reluctant to leave the field and Alderman, hit from behind by one of those running backwards and forwards, reacted by giving chase to his assailant. Moreover, he launched himself into a flying rugby tackle and managed to bring the man down, but in doing so he dislocated his own right shoulder so badly that he missed the whole of the rest of the Australian season.

Alderman, stretchered off, admitted afterwards that he had been foolish to get involved in an incident which led to 26 arrests being made and Greg Chappell, the Australian captain, deciding to take his team from the field for fourteen minutes. The injury also had an effect on his career; he was highly successful again, notably when taking 41 wickets in six Tests to spearhead Australia's regaining of the Ashes in 1989, but his skilful seam and swing bowling nevertheless lost a little of its natural pace and 'nip' following the operation which was needed to help to mend the shoulder.

Alderman had also taken 42 wickets at low cost in the 1981 series in England, but the uncertainty of his long-term future following the self-induced shoulder injury may well have been a factor in the Western Australian's decision to decline a place on the 1985 Ashes tour in order to take the sizeable cheque which came with representing an unofficial 'rebel' Australian team on a visit to South Africa.

SO NEAR AND YET SO FAR FOR HEROIC LAST PAIR

England's only victory in the 1982–83 series came thrillingly by just three runs at Melbourne. But, in the course of a last-wicket partnership of 70 that all but turned the fourth Test Australia's way, Allan Border and Jeff Thomson refused to run a total of 29 comfortable singles.

The reason for this apparent nonsense was purely tactical. And it was a tactical approach that, actually, got them so close to glorious victory.

A tense, tighly fought contest was at last looking as if it was bound to go England's way as Australia, from 171 for 3, collapsed to 218 for 9. Norman Cowans, the Middlesex fast bowler in his first Test series, was the man doing most of the damage with six wickets and Border, who had come in at number six, seemed woefully out of form. England, however, content to get last man Thomson on strike as often as possible, began to allow Border to take singles. With the field set deep, he declined most of them, but some he took and – gradually – his touch began to reappear.

Thomson, meanwhile, was hanging on in determined fashion and, of course, the redoubtable fast bowler was anything but a rabbit with the bat. In the end, as their partnership went past the two-hour mark and into the fifth day, England's tactics were the ones beginning to look shaky.

Amid scenes of high excitement, in a match in which all four innings totals (England 284 and 294; Australia 287 and 288) were within ten runs of each other for the first time in Test history, Thomson edged a ball from Ian Botham to Chris Tavare in the slips. Tavare, to his horror, juggled the chance – but Geoff Miller, running around behind him, grabbed the loose ball and Thomson was out for 21.

The heroic Border was left 62 not out, but at least many more Ashes triumphs were to be his before his great career was brought to a close. In the final Test of this 1982–83 series, too, he scored 89 and 83 to do as much as any Australian to secure the draw which regained the Ashes by a 2–1 margin.

1985

THE STRANGE CASE OF ALLAN LAMB'S BOOT

Controversial umpiring decisions are as much a part of cricket as the dropped catch or the ill-advised stroke; humans are fallible, and mistakes will happen. Every umpire, however, can only call it as he sees it at the time, and in this respect the 'dodgy' decision has just as rightful a place in the fabric of the game as the elegant cover-drive or full-blooded hook.

Take the fifth Test of the 1985 Ashes series, at Edgbaston. The series was locked at 1–1, with Australia as holders having at that stage the narrow advantage in the ongoing battle for the Ashes. There were two Tests left to be played, but the sheer vivacity of England's batting when they came to reply to Australia's first innings of 335 seemed to indicate that they felt their best chance was in the here and now.

Tim Robinson and David Gower put on 331 for the second wicket, with Gower scoring a sumptuous 215, and then Mike Gatting came in to hit a quickfire 100 not out to speed England to a fourth-evening declaration at 595 for 5. By the close, with Richard Ellison taking four wickets with the new ball, Australia were facing almost certain defeat at 37 for 5.

The final morning of the match, however, provided another of cricket's all too familiar twists: it rained. And, after play had finally restarted at 2.30 p.m., Australia's sixth-wicket pair of Greg Ritchie and Wayne Phillips looked up for the fight. They added 77, and there were just 20 minutes left before the start of the compulsory last 20 overs when 'it' happened.

The left-handed Phillips, who had played exceptionally well for his 59, stepped back and hammered a ball from Phil Edmonds down into the ground towards silly point. Allan Lamb, fielding in that close-in position, tried to twist his body around in instinctive self-defence, and the ball seemed to strike him on the instep of his boot and rebound up into the air.

Gower, also fielding close in on the offside, grabbed the looping ball and appealed. David Shepherd, the umpire at the bowlers' end, consulted with his colleague at square leg, David Constant, and gave Phillips out.

The Australians were incensed, although they were forced to direct much of their anger at their dressing room wall. Allan Border, their captain, insisted afterwards that the batsman should have been given the benefit of the doubt – on the basis that no naked human eye could have known for sure that the ball had not touched the ground too before flying up off Lamb's boot. Border later said: 'I considered it rough justice indeed. I have watched that incident from twenty or more angles on all sorts of slow-motion replays and I remain unconvinced that it was a legitimate catch. And if the replays were unconvincing, how the hell could either umpire reasonably adjudicate with the naked eye? But they deemed Phillips out, and with him went our last chance of salvaging a draw. I've relived this incident a hundred times since and wondered what might have been had Phillips survived that appeal.'

Australia, without the rain, must surely have lost the game anyway – but Phillips' misfortune was particularly cruel given the way he and Ritchie had responded to the new hope that the bad weather had given them. As it was, England quickly wrapped up the Australian second innings for 142, just 48 minutes after Phillips had been given out. This win, by an innings and 118 runs, was followed up by another English innings victory in the final Test at the Oval, and the Ashes were suddenly back in England's hands by a 3–1 margin.

Yet, with the Phillips controversy, the thin dividing line between success and failure had been shown up in the sharpest relief once more.

1986-87

JACK WHO?

A member of the select band of Cornishmen to have played cricket for England, the story of Jack Richards is perhaps the most curious.

Of the eight English players to have appeared in all five Tests of the 1986–87 Ashes series, Richards' name would be the one most quiz participants would struggle to remember; indeed, he only ever played in three more Test matches in a career which abruptly ended less than eighteen months after the end of England's triumphant return from Australia as winners of the Ashes themselves, the one-day Perth Challenge tournament, and the World Series Cup. Yet, on that tour, wicket-keeper Richards' batting contributions – which included a magnificent 133 in the second Test in Perth – and some remarkable catching behind the stumps played a significant part in the success of Mike Gatting's team.

Clifton James Richards was born in Penzance, and learned his cricket at the Cornish town's club before being given a trial by Surrey as a teenager. He joined the county's staff in 1976, at the age of seventeen, and two years later he had won a place behind the stumps in the Surrey first team. His batting talents developed later, and in his entire first-class career he was to make only eight centuries.

First selected for England as Bob Taylor's understudy on the 1981–82 tour of India and Sri Lanka, he nevertheless had to wait until 1986 – when he topped 1,000 first-class runs in a season for the first time – to gain international honours. Those two one-day caps against New Zealand led to Ashes tour selection, and it was his superior batting ability (plus England's general lack of batting form in the warm-up matches) which brought Richards his Test debut in the opening game of the series at Brisbane.

He made a duck in his only innings, clean bowled by a swinging full toss, but England were boosted by Ian Botham's cavalier 138, and their first-innings total of 456 was enough to bring them eventual victory and a 1–0 lead. Then, for Richards, came his biggest moment in the sun.

Coming in on day two with England already on 339 for 5, following an opening stand of 223 between Chris Broad and Bill Athey, he and David Gower both hit hundreds and put on a further 207. Richards, never a man lacking in self-confidence, was in truth the more aggressive of the pair – and Gower, remarkably for one of England's greatest and most fluent of batsmen, was mainly content to take a back seat as the Cornishman went for his strokes and found the boundary sixteen times.

This Test, however, was drawn – as was the following one – and Richards' next big contribution came on Boxing Day when he took five catches in Australia's first-innings collapse to 141 all out in a dramatic opening to the fourth Test. One of those efforts was a memorable catch taken on the run over his shoulder as he sprinted fully 30 yards towards the deep square leg boundary after Craig McDermott had skied an attempted hook at Botham.

Victory in Melbourne, completed by an innings and fourteen runs on the third day following another fine century by Broad, gave England an unassailable 2–0 series lead and made sure the Ashes remained theirs. Richards, however, had lost his place to Nottinghamshire's Bruce French by the end of the World Series and played just one Test in the summer of 1987. In 1988 he was recalled to play two more Tests, against the West Indies, but made just thirteen runs from his four innings in those games and was dropped.

Surrey, meanwhile, chose to sever their thirteen-year link with Richards when the 1988 summer (and his existing contract) came to a close. Unable to find another county – and with his reputation for plain speaking possibly counting against him – Richards decided to quit first-class cricket and emigrate to Holland with his Dutch wife.

PETER WHO?

When Australia's team for the final Test of the 1986–87 series was announced, this was the only question on the lips of press and public alike. Even the local Sydney-based Australian cricket writers had hardly heard of Peter Taylor, a 30-year-old off-spinner and lower-order batsman from the city's Northern District club who had played just six first-class matches in his life. Only one of those, too, had come in that current season but Greg Chappell, the Australian chairman of selectors, said the 'unknown' Taylor had been called up to play in the Sydney Test mainly on the strength of an eye-catching performance at the SCG for New South Wales in the previous season's Sheffield Shield final against Queensland.

Initially, though, Taylor's selection was greeted everywhere with 'Peter Who?' headlines, and there were serious suggestions (quickly refuted, of course) that his call-up was the result of a selectorial crossing of wires.

The chosen Test squad, it was quickly noted, contained just one specialist opening batsman – Geoff Marsh – and so it was rumoured that the selectors had intended instead to send for Mark Taylor, the left-handed New South Wales opener who was making mountains of runs for the state at the time and was, of course, destined for a long and successful Test career as run-getter, slip fielder supreme, and subsequently one of Australia's finest captains. But Peter Taylor it was who turned up to play at the SCG and, in one of the greatest 'Boy's Own' stories in sporting history, 'Peter Who' soon became Peter Somebody.

He scored just 11 in Australia's first innings but then, in England's reply, took a remarkable 6 for 78 in 26 overs of controlled and intelligent off-break bowling. He showed that he could bat more than usefully too, as well as spin the ball sharply, when he continued his astonishing Test debut by playing the most important supporting innings of the match when Australia batted again.

Coming in at 145 for 7, with his side just 213 ahead, he batted with great good sense and no little skill to score 42 and help Steve Waugh, who made 73, to add a priceless 98 for the eighth wicket. In all, Taylor batted for more than four hours in the match, having supported century-maker Dean Jones staunchly in the first innings, and it was his second-innings runs in particular which, in the end, proved crucial to Australia's eventual 55-run winning margin.

Taylor took two more English wickets in their second-innings 264, this time letting senior spinner Peter Sleep do most of the damage on the wearing pitch, but his scalps were still the prime ones of Lamb and Botham (both for the second time in the game). Taylor, unsurprisingly given that he was by now a new national hero, was named man of the match.

Four of Taylor's nine home Test appearances were in his familiar surroundings of Sydney, but he never hit the same heights as in his sensational 'debut from nowhere' and his eventual tally of thirteen Tests brought him just 27 wickets at a cost of just under 40 runs apiece.

So was his original selection a case of mistaken identity? Well, whatever the truth of the rumours that it was, Taylor also went on to play in 83 one-day internationals for Australia and become, in the words of national team coach Bobby Simpson, 'the best one-day spin bowler in the world'. Not bad for a 'nobody'.

1989

AUSTRALIA WIN THE NUMBERS GAME

To the uninitiated, it looks an unfair fight: England's 29 versus Australia's 12. In reality, it was the other way around. With a severe 4–0 thrashing of an unsettled, unhappy England, Allan Border's tightly knit Australians ripped back the Ashes in 1989 after all the pundits had beforehand predicted a knife-edge contest.

England were in some disarray right from the start of the summer, when it emerged that David Gower had only been recalled to the captaincy after the appointment of Mike Gatting – the original recommendation of Ted Dexter's selection committee – had been vetoed by Ossie Wheatley, the Test and County Cricket Board's cricket committee chairman.

Dexter was criticised for leaving Headingley, the scene of England's first-Test defeat, just when the last-day crisis was mounting, and Gower's laid-back image took a battering when he stormed out of a Saturday night press conference at the end of a poor third day for England in the second Test at Lord's. Gower, who was becoming rattled at criticism of his captaincy in the field from former players in the media ranks, suddenly stood up and announced he had a taxi to catch if he was to get to the start of a West End theatre preview showing of the Cole Porter musical *Anything Goes*, to which he had been invited.

Then, as the series progressed, English woes were exacerbated by the strengthening rumours and subsequent confirmation that a 'rebel' England side to be led by Gatting had been recruited to tour South Africa in the coming winter.

Indeed, the official news that this unsanctioned tour was going ahead was broken on the very day, at Old Trafford, that England surrendered the Ashes by losing the fourth Test. Three players who had chosen to forsake their Test careers to go to South Africa were in that beaten England side: John Emburey, Neil Foster and Tim Robinson. A fourth, Graham Dilley, had been selected for the match but had been declared unfit just before the start and five others – Chris Broad, Paul Jarvis, Phil DeFreitas, Kim Barnett and Gatting himself – had also by then figured in the 1989 series. At Old Trafford, not even courageous hundreds by Robin Smith and Jack Russell could save English cricket from humiliation both on and off the field.

Ten Australians played in all six Tests of the series, and their only departure from a settled XI came when Greg Campbell, the Tasmanian seamer, played in the opening game at Headingley before giving way to leg-spinner Trevor Hohns. In contrast to the five successive unchanged teams which Border then led to Ashes glory, England had just two players – skipper Gower and wicket-keeper Russell – who appeared in all six Tests. None of the players who chose to go on the rebel tour were selected for England again that summer (they were actually banned for three years). The full list of England's 1989 series participants: Atherton, Barnett, Botham, Broad, Capel, N Cook, Curtis, DeFreitas, Dilley, Emburey, Foster, Fraser, Gatting, Gooch, Gower, Hemmings, Igglesden, Jarvis, Lamb, Moxon, Malcolm, Newport, Pringle, Robinson, Russell, Small, R Smith, Stephenson, Tavare.

1990–91

A TALE OF TWO TIGER MOTHS

England's tour to Australia in 1990–91 was plagued by injury and misfortune but also, under the continuous work ethic demanded of the players by the management of Graham Gooch and Micky Stewart, by an overwhelming joylessness.

The five-match Ashes series was lost 3–0. England were constantly undermined by injuries to their most important players – including skipper Gooch himself – and only one first-class victory was achieved on the entire tour. It was ironic in the extreme, then, that this win should come in a match against Queensland which contained the off-the-field incident that will forever be associated with England's 1990–91 Ashes campaign.

With the Ashes already lost, after defeats at Brisbane and Melbourne and a draw at Sydney, England were glad of their ten-wicket win at Carrara after also losing to New South Wales at Albury in their previous match. But the shaft of light provided by this success against Queensland was almost immediately snuffed out by the management's reaction to a prank with which David Gower and John Morris had tried to lighten the mood.

After their dismissals in England's first innings against Queensland – Morris after a brilliant 132 – the two batsmen had left the ground to be taken up in a pair of 1938 Tiger Moths. This was a particular tourist attraction in the small country town of Carrara, and by this stage of the tour former England captain Gower especially was becoming fed up with the 'all work, no play' mantra of the management team. With

Robin Smith and Allan Lamb by now well set at the crease in a partnership that was to raise a further 108 runs, he persuaded Morris to accompany him on a little flying jaunt.

As they circled the skies above Carrara in their hired planes, it was noticed that on the cricket ground below Smith had just completed his century. Motioning to the pilots that they wanted to go lower, Gower and Morris then buzzed the stadium – the two little biplanes passing lower than the flood-light pylons stationed at each corner of the playing arena. Smith and Lamb, who were in mid-pitch celebration of Smith's hundred at the time, waved back as their team-mates signalled their own appreciation.

Later, when certain members of the English press got wind of the stunt, Gower and Morris even returned to the airfield base – which was close to the ground – in order to pose for smiling and jokey photographs next to the planes in goggles and flying jackets. Later still, however, when England's management were also told by the media of the 'Biggles' escapade, there was a complete absence of jollity. Gower and Morris were summoned to explain themselves, and each ended up being fined £1,000. Morris never added to his three Test caps of the previous English summer, and Gower only played a handful of times more for his country.

As *Wisden* states: 'For all their dereliction of duty in leaving without permission a game in which they were playing, it was a harsh penalty for an essentially light-hearted prank, reflecting all too accurately the joyless nature of the tour. Impressive as Gooch's captaincy was, a hair shirt was usually to be found hanging in his wardrobe.'

1993

ENGLAND PAY BIG PENALTY FOR GOOCH'S HANDBALL

In the popular version of the story of the 1993 Ashes series, it was the 'Ball of the Century' from Shane Warne to Mike Gatting which led to the undermining of England's confidence and the continued mastery of Allan Border's Australians.

There is no denying it had a sizeable effect, of course, with Gatting going for 4 to leave England 80 for 2 in reply to Australia's first innings 289 in the opening Test at Old Trafford. It was Warne's first ball in Test cricket in England, and his first ball in an Ashes contest. It was a big-spinning leg-break which swerved late into Gatting and pitched six inches outside the line of his leg stump before turning viciously across his half-cocked front pad to clip the top of off stump. The look of astonishment on Gatting's face, as well as the ball itself, has quite rightly passed into cricketing legend.

Yet was this, really, the moment that the outcome of the Ashes series was decided? More likely, in actual fact, was the second freakish incident of the match – Graham Gooch's dismissal on the final afternoon.

Gooch, by that stage, had made 133 and was looking in complete control of a situation which had demanded that he lead England's quest for a draw. The pitch was slow, though still taking spin, and even Warne needed to bowl 49 overs to earn his four English second-innings wickets. Gooch, however, and England, paid the ultimate penalty when the captain was quite correctly given out 'handled the ball' for stupidly flicking away with his glove a ball from fast bowler Merv Hughes that had looped up after striking him on the arm. The ball seemed to be dropping towards his stumps, but Gooch could have used his bat to swat it away if he had reacted quickly enough.

As it was, he became only the fifth cricketer in all Tests – and the first Englishman – to be dismissed in this fashion, and his exit during the afternoon session was the real reason why England then slipped to defeat. The end came with just 58 balls of the match remaining. If Gooch had not handed his wicket to the Australians, the match would surely have been drawn.

But, with this result, a downward spiral which had begun for England with their four Test defeats out of four in India and Sri Lanka the previous winter, gathered pace anew. Before too long, moreover, with Australia going 3–0 up after four Tests and then 4–0 up after five, England had seen the resignations both of Gooch and Ted Dexter, the chairman of selectors.

1994-95

THE INJURY JINX THAT EVEN CLAIMED THE PHYSIO

England seemed doomed to suffer a plague of injuries throughout the 1990s on their tours to Australia. In 1990–91 only a handful of the original squad had avoided injury, and three replacement or covering players – Phil DeFreitas, Hugh Morris and Phil Newport – had to be flown out. By the end of the 1994–95 tour, however, skipper Mike Atherton and his men simply had to shake their heads and smile weakly at the catalogue of misfortune that had engulfed them. Otherwise, they would have cried.

Six players from the original sixteen-man squad were forced out of the tour at some stage by injury: Alec Stewart (broken finger), Graeme Hick (slipped disc), Darren Gough (fractured foot), Martin McCague (shin stress fracture), Craig White (torn side muscle) and Shaun Udal (another torn side muscle). Devon Malcolm, England's fast-bowling spearhead who had shattered the South African batting by taking 9 for 57 at the Oval just three months earlier, had to pull out of the crucial first Test with chicken pox. This illness also sidelined reserve seamer Joey Benjamin (although he was at first thought to have shingles) and other injury-affected players during the trip were Atherton (back), Graham Thorpe (adductor muscle), Phil DeFreitas (groin and hamstring) and John Crawley (calf).

The tour really descended into black humour, though, when physiotherapist Dave Roberts suffered a broken finger when taking part in a fielding practice session.

No fewer than six replacement players were flown in to reinforce the creaking squad at varying stages, with Angus Fraser, Chris Lewis and Mark Ramprakash all figuring in the Ashes series itself. Of the other replacements, Jack Russell and Mark Ilott had only brief stays but Neil Fairbrother played in the World Series one-day tournament before – yes, you guessed it – falling awkwardly on his right shoulder and being unable to see out the rest of the tour.

Of the original sixteen, in fact, the only four who remained injury or illness free and were available for selection in every tour match were the chain-smoking Phil Tufnell, the wicket-keeper Steve Rhodes, the 41-year-old Graham Gooch and the 37-year-old Mike Gatting. Of these, Gooch and Gatting were destined to retire from international cricket at the end of what both later admitted had been 'a tour too far' for their ageing bones, while the Middlesex spinner had problems of his own.

After apparently suffering a nervous breakdown due to the stresses of his private life, Tufnell had been booked into the psychiatric unit of the hospital in Perth for 'overnight observation'. Just an hour later, when a psychiatrist attempted to ask Tuffers about his childhood, he decided to make a run for it. In the end, as the doctor chased after him, Tufnell stopped to tell him he was fine and that he wanted to order a taxi to take himself back to the England team hotel. After buying himself a bottle of lager and a packet of cigarettes from the hotel bar, Tufnell interrupted a management meeting to tell them he was back on the tour and feeling fine; the management were at that moment preparing to send back a message asking for Kent's slow left-armer Min Patel to be called up as a replacement.

England, by the way, lost the series 3–1 and, after their return home, team manager Keith Fletcher became the final casualty: halfway through a five-year contract, he was sacked.

1997

SMITH LEFT TO RUE LEEDS PANTOMIME

It is hard to know who felt more aggrieved at the end of Australia's crushing victory in the fourth Test at Headingley – Mike Smith, the Gloucestershire seamer who endured cruel luck in what was to be his sole England appearance, or the man playing the back end of a pantomime cow who had needed hospital treatment after being crash-tackled to the ground by an over-aggressive steward after play on the third evening.

The Yorkshire club had employed rugby-playing 'security' stewards in a bid to keep under control the sometimes over-raucous behaviour on the ground's Western Terrace. Central to that part of the ground's fun (apart from copious quantities of beer) was the by now traditional fancy-dress day on the Saturday. Unfortunately, however, things got a little out of hand when the stewards took it upon themselves to stop spectators cavorting on the outfield at the close of play.

The man at the rear end of the cow, Branco Risek, was hurt as he and his 'other half' attempted to take a little run around the boundary. Meanwhile, another man dressed as a carrot was frog-marched out of the ground for alleged 'drunken and abusive behaviour'. University lecturer Brian Cheesman, who said he had been attending Headingley Tests in fancy dress for fifteen years, strongly denied the charge.

Amid all this mayhem, plus what was happening out in the middle, left-armer Smith must have felt that Test cricket was something of a madhouse. Bowled by Jason Gillespie for 0 at the end of England's first-innings slide to 172 all out, Smith then came on for his first England bowl with Australia in trouble themselves after incisive new-ball bursts by Darren Gough and Dean Headley.

At 50 for 4, in the eighteenth over of their reply, Australia had also lost their four most senior batsmen. Ricky Ponting, then 22 and in his first Ashes Test, came in to join opener Matthew Elliott, himself only 25 and relatively inexperienced at this level.

But Elliott, on 29 and with Australia's total still just 50, enjoyed the huge stroke of luck which was to confirm the destiny of the Ashes and which was to haunt Smith for ever. Fencing at a delivery which straightened up at him off the pitch, Elliott steered the ball straight into the hands of Graham Thorpe at first slip. It looked a regulation catch, but it was dropped. Smith could not believe it, and nor could Australia's two young batsmen believe their good fortune.

Seizing the moment, they reacted to this lapse by counter-attacking furiously – and suddenly England's chance of staying in an Ashes battle they had started so dramatically with victory in the opening Test at Edgbaston was gone. Elliott eventually made 199 and Ponting 127; they put on 268 for the fifth wicket and Australia went on to add an innings win here to the victory in the previous Test at Old Trafford with which they had squared the series.

Smith finished with figures of 0 for 89 from the only 23 overs he ever bowled in the Test arena and, like the men dressed up as a pantomime cow and the man in the carrot costume, had to be content with playing merely a walk-on part in the ongoing epic that is Ashes cricket.

Australia, meanwhile, won the fifth Test too, at Trent Bridge, before England pegged their winning margin back to 3–2 with victory in a low-scoring but highly exciting final match of the series at the Oval.

1998–99

HERO HEADLEY STILL FUMING OVER RUN-OUT DECISION

Former England fast bowler Dean Headley is a unique cricketer, and not just because he is the only grandson of a West Indian batting legend to have won an Ashes Test for England. He is the third member of the only cricketing family to have produced Test players in a direct line from grandfather to father to son.

'I may not have been a better batsman than my dad, let alone my grandad,' Dean is fond of saying, when quizzed about comparisons between himself, father Ron, and grandfather George, 'but I was a better bowler than either of them!'

A stress fracture of the back sadly cut short Headley's international career in its prime, after he had taken 60 wickets from fifteen Tests at an average of 27.85, but at least he had the glory of his match-winning 6 for 60 at Melbourne in late December 1998 to take with him into retirement at the age of 30. Headley, however, reckons he would have spearheaded England to another victory in Sydney the following week had it not been for one of the most controversial umpiring decisions of modern times.

England's astounding twelve-run win in Melbourne, when Headley and Darren Gough bowled Australia out for 162 at the end of the longest day and longest session in Test history, may not have been enough to save the Ashes (England were then 2–1 down in the series with one match to play), but it should, according to Headley, have led to an England fightback to a creditable 2–2 draw and put an end to the dominance Australia had enjoyed since 1989.

England went into the fifth Test at Sydney on a high, despite the loss of opener Mike Atherton to a debilitating back injury. A brilliant catch at square leg by Mark Ramprakash, from a fierce Justin Langer pull at Alan Mullally, and a spell of 4 for 4 in thirteen balls by Headley, had reduced Australia from 103 for 2 to 140 for 7 as they chased 175 for victory in Melbourne. Headley, with another wicket, and Gough, with the last two, had then ensured that Australia's heavy stumble in sight of the finishing line became a flat-out fall. And all this had taken place in a final session which stretched just beyond four hours because, first, of an early tea, and, second, because Australian captain Steve Waugh had claimed the extra half hour at 7.22 p.m. when his side were just fourteen runs away from winning.

Now, in Sydney, in a Test which began just four days later, Mark Waugh's sixteenth Test hundred gave Australia an early advantage that was countered when Gough removed Ian Healy, Stuart MacGill and Colin Miller in successive deliveries to claim England's first Ashes hat-trick since Jack Hearne at Headingley in 1899. England, despite being 102 in arrears on first innings, then bowled Australia out for just 184 in their second innings with Headley adding four more wickets to take his match haul to 8 for 102. And yet, Headley believes, Australia should not have got even close to 184.

Opener Michael Slater, who scored 123 of the total – a near record 66.84 per cent of it – seemed to be beaten by Headley's direct-hit throw when he had made just 35. It would have left Australia 60 for 3, but umpire Steve Dunne, of New Zealand, did not take responsibility for giving the decision. Even Slater took off his batting gloves resignedly.

Dunne referred the verdict to his third umpire colleague Simon Taufel, sitting in the stands in front of a television monitor. Unfortunately for England, though, the stumps were obscured by the bowler, Peter Such, and so no definite conclusion could be reached about whether Slater had made his ground or not. There was no second camera angle available, either, and so Slater survived after being given the benefit of the doubt. He scored 88 more runs and, in the end, Australia won by 98 to finish the series 3–1 winners.

Headley, who now works as development director of award-winning Kent-based publishing and newspaper group Kosmedia, can still be provoked into chuntering on about it today . . .

2001

SUPERMAN WHO SCORED A HUNDRED ON ONE LEG

Long before the end of his great career, Steve Waugh became the only player in the Australian Test side who had actually experienced an Ashes series defeat. Yet, as a senior batsman and captain who seemed to specialise in making England suffer, it was as if Waugh was continually intent on extracting the maximum payback price for this indignity.

Perhaps his most triumphant moment, however, in the nine Ashes series he played from 1986–87 to 2002–03, came at the end of the 2001 rubber, at the Oval. He scored the little matter of 157 not out, for one thing, and presided over an innings victory in this fifth Test which gave his Australia team a 4–1 series win. But it was what lay behind this personal and overall triumph that makes the feat an extraordinary one.

On 4 August, in the third Test at Trent Bridge, Waugh had pulled a muscle in his left calf as he pushed off from the crease to take his first single. He made it to the other end, but then collapsed in a heap and, after inspection from Errol Alcott, the Australian team physio, he was carried from the field on a stretcher. Soon afterwards, with his twin brother Mark replacing him out in the middle, the Ashes were retained as Australia completed a seven-wicket victory.

What, everyone asked, was Waugh going to do with the remaining few weeks of the series? Put his feet up? Go back home, especially now that the Ashes were his? The muscle tear was diagnosed as being so severe that he was advised at least to rest it. Surely, he couldn't play again on the tour? Everyone should have known better.

Waugh was reportedly wary of flying home, anyway, due to the possibility of a deep vein thrombosis, and so he announced that, instead, he was going to get himself fit for the final Test. But that is less than three weeks away, said friend and foe alike. Yes, replied Waugh, and he smiled his narrow-eyed gunslinger's smile.

With Alcott supervising, Waugh got on with his rehabilitation work, while Adam Gilchrist took over the captaincy and promptly lost the fourth Test at Headingley. Gilchrist made a second-innings declaration that was intended to give Australia the maximum chance of maintaining their bid for a 5–0 whitewash but which only succeeded in allowing Mark Butcher the opportunity to score an unbeaten 173 not out. England, their spirits boosted by Butcher's match-winning brilliance, needed to be taken down a peg or two at the Oval . . . and there was only one man to do it! Despite being far from fully fit, Waugh insisted he was able to play, and promptly won the toss.

By the end of the first day he was at the crease, too, making 12 not out in support of his brother Mark as Australia racked up 324 for 2. The second day brought another deluge of runs for the Aussies, even though Steve could scarcely limp his singles. He seemed literally at times to be dragging his bad leg after him as he ran between the wickets. The captain finally brought both the innings and his own incredible show of physical courage and sheer willpower to a close with the total at 641 for four, both Waughs having reached three figures (Mark's 20th Test hundred, and Steve's 27th). His 100th run, too, provided a never-to-be-forgotten moment in the Ashes story: a scrambled, limping, wincing single that was completed by a dive for the safety of the crease.

Bloody-mindedly, of course, Waugh was not even satisfied with that. He added 57 more unbeaten runs and then spent the three and a bit days left hobbling around out on the field, directing operations from the slips as England were bowled out for 432 and 184 in reply.

2002–03

A GLIMPSE OF A BRIGHTER FUTURE?

England's cricketers, and the millions who follow their progress with a hope that in recent times has often outweighed expectation, believed at the end of the 2002–03 series in Australia that they had seen a shining, bright chink of light in what had become a forbiddingly dark Ashes tunnel. What they glimpsed, with a collective leap of the heart, was a future that did not contain either Glenn McGrath or Shane Warne . . . and it was a future that they liked very much indeed.

The Ashes had already been retained yet again, and the scoreboard after four Tests read: Australia 4 England 0. But, for the final Test at Sydney, there was suddenly new hope for Nasser Hussain and his battered team. For the first time since November 1992, Australia were forced to go into a Test match without their two greatest bowlers – McGrath being forced to sit things out with a side strain and Warne absent with shoulder trouble.

Honours could hardly have been more even after both sides had batted once: England's 362, built upon Butcher's 124 and seventies from both Hussain and Stewart, was passed – just – by Australia's 363, in which Steve Waugh made a memorable and emotional 102 and Gilchrist a superlative 94-ball century.

Now, though, where could Australia turn as Michael Vaughan took command? Jason Gillespie, McGrath's obvious replacement as the enforcer at the head of the pace attack, faded into the background and Stuart MacGill, a fine leg-spinner in his own right but – crucially – not Warne, found that he could not match his genius of a contemporary for control. Vaughan made 183, and with Hussain contributing another gutsy 72 and Stewart a jaunty unbeaten 38, England were even able to declare, at 452 for 9, and see how Australia fared under pressure. Not very well at all, was the answer, and Andy Caddick's 7 for 94 condemned Australia to 226 all out and defeat by 225 runs.

Since 1989, though, when Allan Border wrested back the urn for his country, Australia have won 28 of 43 Ashes Tests . . . and England only seven. Australia's run of eight successive Ashes series victories is their best-ever sequence of success, and has been matched only by the England teams of 1882 to 1890 right at the very beginning of Ashes history. Throughout the magnificent, unmatchable 123-year epic that has been the Ashes story, however, it has been the delicious ebb and flow of cricketing power between the Mother Country and her strong-armed offspring that has proved the most fascinating sub-plot of all.

As the 2005 Ashes series approaches, seemingly more eagerly awaited than for many a year, all England yearns for heroes to rise up and match the deeds of those such as Grace, Barnes, Hobbs, Sutcliffe, Hammond, Larwood, Tyson, Laker, Boycott, Snow, Willis and Botham. Australia, meanwhile, waits to see if McGrath and Warne can add yet more lustre to their own legend and to those of the likes of Spofforth, Armstrong, Gregory, Bradman, Lindwall, Miller, Benaud, Lillee, Thomson, the Chappells and the Waughs. New heroes, of course, will always emerge – and many of them are as yet unborn.

To delve into the pages of the Ashes story, indeed, is to discover so many tales of heroic endeavour and strange and wonderful incident that, if it were presented as a work of mere fiction, you simply would not believe it. Let us hope that the next 100 and more years are no different to all that has gone before!

Ashes Statistics and Results

Overall statistics

There have been 62 Ashes series played
England have held the Ashes a total of 28 times
Australia have held the Ashes a total of 34 times

England have won 27 Ashes series outright
Australia have won 30 Ashes series outright
There have been five drawn series

England have won 93 Ashes Tests
Australia have won 115 Ashes Tests
There have been 82 drawn Ashes Tests

Overall results

Series	Tests	E	A	D	Held by
1882–83	4*	2	2	0	England
1884	3	1	0	2	England
1884–85	5	3	2	0	England
1886	3	3	0	0	England
1886–87	2	2	0	0	England
1887–88	1	1	0	0	England
1888	3	2	1	0	England
1890†	2	2	0	0	England
1891–92	3	1	2	0	Australia
1893	3	1	0	2	England

1894–95	5	3	2	0	England
1896	3	2	1	0	England
1897–98	5	1	4	0	Australia
1899	5	0	1	4	Australia
1901–02	5	1	4	0	Australia
1902	5	1	2	2	Australia
1903–04	5	3	2	0	England
1905	5	2	0	3	England
1907–08	5	1	4	0	Australia
1909	5	1	2	2	Australia
1911–12	5	4	1	0	England
1912	3	1	0	2	England
1920–21	5	0	5	0	Australia
1921	5	0	3	2	Australia
1924–25	5	1	4	0	Australia
1926	5	1	0	4	England
1928–29	5	4	1	0	England
1930	5	1	2	2	Australia
1932–33	5	4	1	0	England
1934	5	1	2	2	Australia
1936–37	5	2	3	0	Australia
1938†	4	1	1	2	Australia
1946–47	5	0	3	2	Australia
1948	5	0	4	1	Australia
1950–51	5	1	4	0	Australia
1953	5	1	0	4	England
1954–55	5	3	1	1	England
1956	5	2	1	2	England
1958–59	5	0	4	1	Australia
1961	5	1	2	2	Australia
1962–63	5	1	1	3	Australia
1964	5	0	1	4	Australia
1965–66	5	1	1	3	Australia
1968	5	1	1	3	Australia
1970–71†	6	2	0	4	England
1972	5	2	2	1	England
1974–75	6	1	4	1	Australia
1975	4	0	1	3	Australia

1977	5	3	0	2	England
1978–79	6	5	1	0	England
1981	6	3	1	2	England
1982–83	5	1	2	2	Australia
1985	6	3	1	2	England
1986–87	5	2	1	2	England
1989	6	0	4	2	Australia
1990–91	5	0	3	2	Australia
1993	6	1	4	1	Australia
1994–95	5	1	3	1	Australia
1997	6	2	3	1	Australia
1998–99	5	1	3	1	Australia
2001	5	1	4	0	Australia
2002–03	5	1	4	0	Australia

* In 1882–83 England won the Ashes 2–1 after a series of three matches, but then an extra game was played which Australia won.

† One Test in each of the 1890, 1938 and 1970–71 series was abandoned without a ball being bowled

England and Australia played nine matches against each other from 1876–77 until 1882, before the Ashes series of matches was created.

England and Australia have played five matches against each other (one in 1976–77, three in 1979–80 and one in 1987–88) in which the Ashes were not at stake.